10/02

D0116145

10/02

☆ The Vietnam War ☆

A HISTORY OF U.S. INVOLVEMENT

Titles in The American War Library series include:

World War II
Hitler and the Nazis
Kamikazes
Leaders and Generals
Life as a POW
Life of an American Soldier in
  Europe
Strategic Battles in Europe
Strategic Battles in the Pacific
The War at Home
Weapons of War

The Civil War
Leaders of the North and South
Life Among the Soldiers and
  Cavalry
Lincoln and the Abolition of
  Slavery

Strategic Battles
Weapons of War

The Persian Gulf War
Leaders and Generals
Life of an American Soldier
The War Against Iraq
Weapons of War

The Vietnam War
A History of U.S. Involvement
The Home Front: Americans
  Protest the War
Leaders and Generals
Life of an American Soldier
Life as a POW
Weapons of War

AMERICAN
WAR LIBRARY

✯ The Vietnam War ✯

A HISTORY OF U.S. INVOLVEMENT

by John M. Dunn

Lucent Books, P.O. Box 289011, San Diego, CA 92198-9011

Library of Congress Cataloging-in-Publication Data

Dunn, John M., 1949–
    A history of U.S. involvement / by John M. Dunn.
        p. cm.—(American war library. Vietnam War)
    Includes bibliographical references (p.) and index.
        ISBN 1-56006-645-8 (hard cover)
        1. Vietnamese Conflict, 1961–1975—United States—
    Juvenile literature. 2. United States—History—1961–1969—
    Juvenile literature. 3. United States—History—1969—Juvenile
    literature. [1. Vietnamese Conflict, 1961–1975.] I. Title: History of
    United States involvement. II. Title. III. Series.
        DS558 .D86 2001
        959.704'3373—dc21   00-010221

Copyright 2001 by Lucent Books, Inc.
P.O. Box 289011, San Diego, California 92198-9011

Printed in the U.S.A.

★ Contents ★

A Nation Forged by War

The United States, like many nations, was forged and defined by war. Despite Benjamin Franklin's opinion that "There never was a good war or a bad peace," the United States owes its very existence to the War of Independence, one to which Franklin wholeheartedly subscribed. The country forged by war in 1776 was tempered and made stronger by the Civil War in the 1860s.

The Texas Revolution, the Mexican-American War, and the Spanish-American War expanded the country's borders and gave it overseas possessions. These wars made the United States a world power, but this status came with a price, as the nation became a key but reluctant player in both World War I and World War II.

Each successive war further defined the country's role on the world stage. Following World War II, U.S. foreign policy redefined itself to focus on the role of defender, not only of the freedom of its own citizens, but also of the freedom of people everywhere. During the cold war that followed World War II until the collapse of the Soviet Union, defending the world meant fighting communism. This goal, manifested in the Korean and Vietnam conflicts, proved elusive, and soured the American public on its achievability. As the United States emerged as the world's sole superpower, American foreign policy has been guided less by national interest and more on protecting international human rights. But as involvement in Somalia and Kosovo prove, this goal has been equally elusive.

As a result, the country's view of itself changed. Bolstered by victories in World Wars I and II, Americans first relished the role of protector. But, as war followed war in a seemingly endless procession, Americans began to doubt their leaders, their motives, and themselves. The Vietnam War especially caused people to question the validity of sending its young people to die in places where they were not particularly wanted and for people who did not seem especially grateful.

While the most obvious changes brought about by America's wars have been geopolitical in nature, many other aspects of society have been touched. War often does not bring about change directly, but acts instead like the catalyst in a chemical reaction, accelerating changes already in progress.

Some of these changes have been societal. The role of women in the United States had been slowly changing, but World War II put thousands into the workforce and into uniform. They might have gone back to being housewives after the war, but equality, once experienced, would not be forgotten.

Likewise, wars have accelerated technological change. The necessity for faster airplanes and a more destructive bomb led to the development of jet planes and nuclear energy. Artificial fibers developed for parachutes in the 1940s were used in the clothing of the 1950s.

Lucent Books' American War Library covers key wars in the development of the nation. Each war is covered in several volumes, to allow for more detail, context, and to provide volumes on often neglected subjects, such as the kamikazes of World War II, or weapons used in the Civil War. As with all Lucent Books, notes, annotated bibliographies, and appendixes such as glossaries give students a launching point for further research. In addition, sidebars and archival photographs enhance the text. Together, each volume in The American War Library will aid students in understanding how America's wars have shaped and changed its politics, economics, and society.

America's Longest War

For more than two decades, 2.5 million American airmen, sailors, and soldiers at different times found themselves embroiled in a civil war in a distant and divided land in Southeast Asia. The Americans faced two main enemies: the North Vietnamese and their Communist allies, the Vietcong, who waged guerrilla war in South Vietnam. What motivated these two powers was a burning desire to overthrow the government of South Vietnam and unite North and South Vietnam under the banner of Communism.

The United States opposed this effort. In the post–World War II era, Americans and their allies feared any expansion of Communism—a form of dictatorial government they deemed a threat to world peace. Following a French departure from Vietnam, three American presidents in a row steadily increased the number of American military personnel in South Vietnam. By 1968, six hundred thousand U.S. troops waged war there against the Communists.

But this prolonged campaign exacted a great toll on the American people. Not since the American Civil War had the nation been as divided as it was over the Vietnam War. Supporters of the war claimed American involvement was necessary to check the spread of Communism, an ideology advanced by the totalitarian governments of the People's Republic of China and the Soviet Union. War opponents, however, argued that the United States had no right to take sides in an overseas conflict in Southeast Asia. Many also questioned the legality of a war the U.S. Congress never fully approved as required by the U.S. Constitution. Other critics viewed U.S. military actions as both immoral and a squandering of precious manpower and resources.

The deadly conflict in Vietnam was America's first "television war." As never before, Americans witnessed the graphic horrors of combat on the evening news in their living rooms. These images traumatized the

Four U.S. soldiers lie dead in Vietnam. The war eventually claimed fifty-eight thousand American lives, and left three hundred thousand wounded.

nation and helped fuel a growing antiwar protest movement that ripped the fabric of American society, drove one president from office, and eventually helped end U.S. involvement in Vietnam.

The Vietnam War was also America's longest and costliest war. The country involved itself in varying degrees in Vietnam for more than twenty years; it spent $150 billion. Nearly fifty-eight thousand Americans died in the conflict, and another three hundred thousand were wounded. Many analysts suggest the Vietnam War was also the first war the nation did not win. Others counter this claim by arguing the United States did accomplish its mission—as long as American troops stayed in South Vietnam to provide protection against the Communists. President Richard Nixon contended that his policies "won the war" but that Congress did not honor commitments to South Vietnam and so "lost the peace."[1] When the Americans evacuated Vietnam for good in 1975, Communist forces easily swept into the South and put the entire country under Communist rule.

In the aftermath of war, the United States found itself transformed. No longer did it possess the same confidence that had buoyed the nation during and after World War II. Thirty years after helping to defeat the military juggernauts of Germany, Italy, and Japan, the United States had to face the fact that a poor, backward, yet fiercely determined nation had humbled a superpower.

Like no other American war, the Vietnam War forced Americans to debate why, when, and how they should wage future wars. It also caused them to wonder whether their actions in Vietnam were necessary and right, or tragically wrong.

Chapter 1

The Roots of American Involvement

Bounded by China on the north, Cambodia (Kampuchea) and Laos on the west, and the South China Sea on the south and east, lies the Southeast Asian country called Vietnam. Long and S shaped, sometimes said to resemble a "starving sea horse," Vietnam stretches from north to south for twelve hundred miles.

Vietnam comprises three distinct geographical regions. In North Vietnam a belt of mountain ranges form a ring around the rich delta of the Red River, along which live the majority of the region's population. Most reside in two large urban areas, Hanoi and Haiphong, a seacoast city. Central Vietnam consists of several small plains. South Vietnam is a region of swamps and rice paddies along the Mekong River delta. South Vietnam is also home to Ho Chi Minh City—once called Saigon—Vietnam's largest urban area.

Vietnam has two main seasons—a hot season that lasts from October to May and the rainy monsoon season, which dominates the rest of the year. A combination of warm temperatures and abundant rain produce a lush green canopy across the country in the form of dense forests and jungles thick with an undergrowth of bamboo. Elephants, buffalo, tigers, and panthers range in the remote mountainous areas.

Vietnam boasts a mixture of Asian peoples and cultures. Over the centuries, influences from India, China, and Indonesia merged with native ways of life. From nearby China came Buddhism, Taoism, and Confucianism, the country's main religions. Ancient practices of ancestor and nature worship have also thrived in Vietnam for centuries.

Because of its geographical setting, Vietnam has had to fend off foreign powers during much of its long history. For almost one thousand years (111 B.C to A.D. 938), the Vietnamese fought with differing levels of success to keep Chinese warlords from overpowering them. They also managed to stave off the Portuguese in 1535 and the

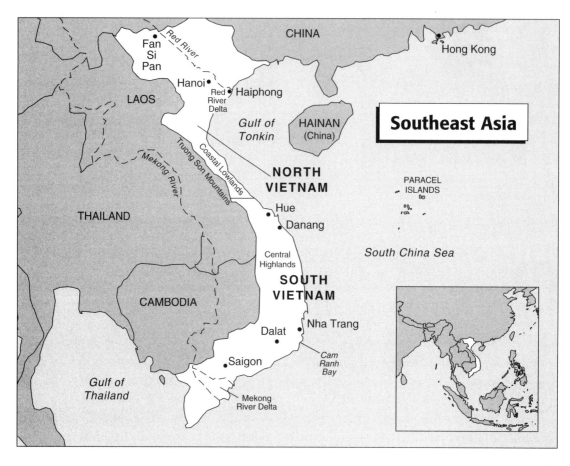

Dutch in 1636. But they failed to keep out the French, who arrived in 1689 to spread Catholicism and open up trade with nearby China.

In time, France wanted more from Vietnam. In 1861, it seized Saigon. By 1887, France controlled Vietnam and its neighbors, Laos and Cambodia, and had united all three into a single political unit called French Indochina.

Although French rule brought some benefits—railroads, highways, seaports, public schools, hospitals, improved health conditions—its main impact on Vietnam was destructive. France took control of Vietnam's economy and military. It imposed the French legal system on the Vietnamese people. Students were forced to learn French at Vietnamese schools. The French also imposed burdensome taxes on the Vietnamese and excluded them from holding the most important government jobs. Though Vietnam's emperor remained on the throne, and the country's ruling classes kept positions of importance, all were subservient to France.

French businessmen dominated Vietnamese mines, rice fields, and coffee, tea, and rubber plantations, and forced thousands of Vietnamese people to work at these places for pennies a day under semislave conditions. Overseers brutally punished anyone who resisted or failed to work hard enough. Worse still, the French conscripted young Vietnamese men and forced them to fight France's wars.

Such unfairness and abuse provoked widespread hatred of the French from the Vietnamese people. Armed rebellion arose many times during almost a century of French imperialism. Almost invariably, French troops smashed these uprisings with little difficulty. France was unable, however, to stamp out one resistance movement that would one day crush French troops in Vietnam. This insurrection was led by Ho Chi Minh—the future dictator of North Vietnam.

The Rise of the Viet Minh

The man destined to become Vietnam's greatest nationalist and revolutionary was born in 1890 with the name of Nguyen Tat Thanh. Later he adopted the name

France's imperialistic rule over Vietnam for nearly a century allowed it control over rice fields (pictured), mines, coffee, tea, and rubber plantations.

that would become known around the world: Ho Chi Minh, or "He Who Enlightens." Ho grew up in Nghe-Trinh province, a region known for spawning political troublemakers and fiery opponents of the French. His father lost an important government job because of his outspoken criticism of the French, and Ho's brother and sister joined anti-French crusades.

At the age of nineteen, Ho left Vietnam as a seaman on a merchant ship and made his way to Europe. There, he worked at odd jobs and joined various Communist and Socialist groups that introduced him to the works of Karl Marx, Friedrich Engels, and other radical thinkers who predicted that exploited workers one day would overthrow the ruling classes of the industrialized nations. In theory, the workers would replace oppressive governments that favored the privileged few with new socialistic governments that would redistribute resources and wealth to all people fairly.

Based on his bitter experiences under French rule, Ho believed Communism offered the best hope for the masses of Vietnamese peasants. He considered the Russian Revolution of 1917 that imposed Communism on the former Russian empire as a model of what could be done in Vietnam. In 1920, he joined the French Communist party. Ten years later, he and fellow revolutionaries formed the Indochinese Communist party in Hong Kong. Ho later became excited by another Communist revolution underway in China in the

Ho Chi Minh became Vietnam's greatest revolutionary leader and advocate for Communism, ending French colonial rule in 1954.

1930s. During this period of his life, "[Ho was a] small, frail young man with a gaunt face and an expression of great gentleness, aglow with the flame which so often burns in the eyes of people who are exalted by an idea," Ho Van Tao, a fellow revolutionary, later recalled.[2]

Ho next spent several years in Russia and China learning all he could about Communism. Then at the outbreak of World War II in 1939, he returned to Vietnam. He believed the time was ripe for revolution, and he was prepared to be the leader who would unify his people and oust the French. "The revolt of the colonial peasant is imminent,"[3] he earlier wrote.

Communism was not Ho Chi Minh's only inspiration. He also admired the American revolutionary leaders who ended British colonial rule in the eighteenth century. Ho even partly fashioned his revolution on the actions and words of George Washington. The Vietnamese revolutionary carried with him a copy of the U.S. Declaration of Independence.

In 1941, Ho organized nationalist-minded young men and women into the League for Vietnam Independence, or the Viet Minh. Though Ho was a Communist, he welcomed all Vietnamese willing to work together to drive the French out of Vietnam. But first he and his Viet Minh followers had to contend with the Japanese who had invaded Southeast Asia in 1940 and temporarily ended French dominance in the area. The Japanese, however, had not come to liberate Vietnam. They came to rule.

So Ho's forces turned against the Japanese. This time they had help from a powerful foe of the Japanese—the United States. American OSS teams (Office of Strategic Services, which later became the Central Intelligence Agency, or CIA) fought side by side with the Vietnamese against the Japanese in the jungles of Vietnam. In August, the Japanese surrendered to the Americans as World War II came to an end.

The Viet Minh occupied Hanoi in North Vietnam, and Ho quickly proclaimed Vietnam an independent nation and himself its provisional president. The Communists also forced Bao Dai, Vietnam's last emperor, to abdicate.

A Vietnamese Declaration of Rights

In his book *A People's History of the United States,* historian Howard Zinn includes this selection of a Declaration of Independence and a list of grievances against the French proclaimed by Ho Chi Minh and his fellow revolutionists at the end of World War II in 1945:

All men are created equal. They are endowed by their Creator with certain inalienable rights; among these are Life, Liberty, and the pursuit of Happiness. . . .

[The French] have enforced inhuman laws. . . . They have built more prisons than schools. They have mercilessly slain our patriots, they have drowned uprisings in rivers of blood. They have fettered public opinion. . . . They have robbed us of our rice fields, our mines, our forests, and our raw materials. . . .

They have invented numerous unjustifiable taxes and reduced our people, especially our peasantry, to a state of extreme poverty. . . .

. . . from the end of last year, to the beginning of this year . . . more than two million of our fellow-citizens died of starvation. . . .

The whole Vietnamese people, animated by a common purpose, are determined to fight to the bitter end against any attempt by the French colonialists to reconquer their country.

But this Communist takeover was limited to Hanoi. With grave disappointment, Ho's forces learned that British troops—allies of the Americans—had occupied Saigon in South Vietnam to maintain order. Worse yet, the British announced they would soon hand over control of Saigon to the French, who had every intention of reasserting their authority over Vietnam.

A Divided Nation

France, however, was not as powerful as it once had been. World War II took many French lives and used much of France's resources. In addition, France could not ignore the fact that a formidable foe now controlled North Vietnam and was in no mood to step down and make way for anyone else to govern.

Nonetheless, France soon managed to reestablish its presence as a military force and set out once again to be the dominant authority in South Vietnam. Aware of the hostility it faced in the North, the French proposed a new political arrangement for Vietnam. The plan gave limited self-government to North Vietnam and called for free elections in South Vietnam to determine its future. But there was a catch—all of Vietnam must remain part of a "French Union."

Though the French proposal was hardly what Ho's followers had in mind, the Communists agreed to talk with French representatives anyway. But when negotiations broke down, Ho's forces relocated to the mountains, determined to use force to oust the hated French in South Vietnam. Soon, the two sides were at war with each other.

To Ho's great and lasting dismay, the United States turned down his repeated requests for aid and official recognition of his authority in North Vietnam. This snub, however, did not mean that American foreign policy officials approved of France's actions in Vietnam. Many, in fact, opposed French recolonization efforts and argued that France was violating a principle of the newly created United Nations: the right of every country to determine its own destiny without foreign interference. In the final months of World War II, American president Franklin D. Roosevelt pointed out that Indochina had been "liberated by American aid and American troops [and] should never be handed back to the French, to be milked by their imperialists."[4]

American criticism of France softened after Roosevelt died in 1945. For one thing, France was an old friend that many American leaders were not eager to offend. This relationship became increasingly important when the Soviet Union occupied many Eastern European nations following the end of World War II. American strategists saw the Soviet aggression as a new threat to world peace. They also considered France a major democratic power that was strong enough to resist Soviet aggression in war-torn Western Europe. To keep their old ally happy and useful to American interests, U.S. officials ceased publicly criticizing the French, even when their actions in Vietnam turned into a war against North Vietnam.

Vietnam's Growing Importance

France's presence in Vietnam became even more important to the United States when Communist expansion intensified in the late 1940s. By now many officials believed that Soviet-style Communism represented not just a European, but a global threat. Adding to the worries, China fell to Communist revolutionaries in 1949. A year later Communist forces in North Korea threatened to take over

French soldiers interrogate a Vietnamese. The French reestablished their military presence in Vietnam after the British handed over control of Saigon at the end of World War II.

South Korea. All these events prompted some U.S. officials to wonder if more was going on in Vietnam than just a struggle against renewed colonialism. Some speculated that North Vietnam was being manipulated behind the scenes by the Soviet Union or Red China. Though there was little, if any, proof that North Vietnam was a pawn of these major Communist nations, it did receive military and financial aid from both. In response to these troubling events, President Harry Truman officially recognized the French-supported government of South Vietnam on February 7, 1950. Months later, the United States sent military aid to South Vietnam for the first time.

America's switch from neutrality to active assistance was meant to contain Communism from spreading any farther in Asia. If one country fell to the Communists, went a popular argument at the time, neighboring countries were sure to follow. In April 1954, Truman's successor, President Dwight Eisenhower, explained the idea this way: "You have a row of dominoes set up. You knock over the first one, and what will happen to the last one is a certainty that it will go over very quickly. So you could have a beginning of a disintegration that would have the most profound consequences."[5] Based on this fear, many U.S. policy makers favored American intervention in Southeast Asia.

Other American officials balked at this idea. Analysts for the CIA, for example, believed that the United States faced great

risks by becoming involved in Vietnam. They pointed out that popular support for South Vietnam's government was weak. In addition, they argued, Vietnam's Communist forces were powerful, motivated, determined, and experienced. Despite these risks, the Eisenhower administration decided to beef up American assistance to South Vietnam with financial aid. Ultimately, the United States paid 75 percent of France's war costs.

Even with American help, the war went badly for the French. Time and time again, Ho Chi Minh's troops successfully used guerrilla warfare techniques—such as sniping, sabotage, and hit-and-run tactics—to outmaneuver their enemy. In contrast, French officers tended to rely on big battle

Ho Chi Minh Sizes Up His Errors

In his book *Vietnam: A History,* Vietnam War correspondent and author Stanley Karnow provides a portion of Ho Chi Minh's 1945 statement of self-criticism.

Though five months have passed since we declared independence, no foreign countries have recognized us. Though our soldiers have fought gloriously, we are still far from victory. Though our administration is honest and efficient, corruption has not been eliminated. Though we have introduced reforms, disorder disturbs several areas. We could ascribe these setbacks to the fact that our regime is young, or make other excuses. But no. Our successes are due to the efforts of our citizens, and our shortcomings are our own fault.

tactics they employed in World War II. But these actions were less effective in Vietnam. Ho's forces also knew the terrain better than the French. In addition, their hatred of the French, dedication to the cause of Communism, and a burning desire to be free of foreign control made them a daunting enemy. Communist leaders were also willing to make great sacrifices to win. "You will kill ten of our men, and we will kill one of yours, and in the end it will be you who tire of it,"[6] Ho told the French in 1946.

On May 7, 1954, a turning point in the struggle occurred when Viet Minh forces under the command of General Vo Nguyen Giap defeated the French after a fifty-six-day battle at Dien Bien Phu in northwest Vietnam. After this crippling defeat, public support in France for the war evaporated. Growing numbers of French people demanded their government pull out of Vietnam forever.

Despite their own country's earlier objections to France's recolonization attempts, many American officials, who feared the growth of Communism, now opposed a French pullout from Vietnam. Members of the U.S. National Security Council (NSC) even stood against a negotiated settlement. Instead, they insisted that nothing short of military victory over the North Vietnamese could keep Communism from spreading.

But the French were ready to negotiate a settlement. They attended a peace conference in Geneva, Switzerland, cochaired by Great Britain and the Soviet Union, to discuss the terms of a cease-fire in Vietnam. There they were joined by representatives from China, the Soviet Union, the United States, and leaders from North and South Vietnam.

According to the agreement hammered out in Geneva, the former French colony was broken up into four areas. Once again Laos and Cambodia became separate nations. Vietnam was divided along the 17th parallel, with the Saigon government in control of the South and Ho Chi Minh's Communists commanding the North.

But the division of Vietnam was only meant to be temporary. The 1954 Geneva peace agreement also stipulated that a nationwide election be held in 1956 to enable the Vietnamese people to decide their country's future. Though North Vietnamese leaders initially opposed this provision, they soon realized that since North Vietnam was more populated than the South, the upcoming election offered them a good chance to unite the nation under Communist rule. Until that day arrived, Ho began brutally transforming North Vietnam into a totalitarian Communist regime. This meant the Communists regulated every aspect of daily life—politics, economics, education—with absolute control.

Meanwhile, American officials worried. They had serious doubts about the ability of South Vietnam's current leader—Bao Dai, the former emperor of Vietnam whom the French now had installed as chief of

An Untimely Letter

In Jules Roy's *The Battle of Dienbienphu* appears this portion of a letter written by a French second lieutenant named Thelot. Thelot was killed at Dien Bien Phu by the time the letter reached his brother.

The guns are spitting much less and have withdrawn into the mountains, but the Viets are very close to us in the basin. Now and then I can make out a few through my field glasses. They haven't attacked our strong point yet, but they have come and left leaflets on our barbed-wire defenses. Write to me at S.P.54,640. Your letters will reach me, for mail is forwarded everywhere without fail; it is dropped to us with our provisions. Reassure our parents. Morale here could not be better.

French soldiers dodge an explosion at Dien Bien Phu in April 1954.

state of South Vietnam. They were also disturbed that a power vacuum was being created in South Vietnam by the departure of the French. U.S. officials had no doubts that the more populous North Vietnam would win any election. These concerns caused many Americans to wonder if the United States would use military power to prevent a Communist takeover.

On March 10, 1953, Eisenhower offered a response: "I will say this: there is going to be no involvement of America in war unless it is a result of the constitutional process that is placed upon Congress to declare it. Now, let us have that clear; and that is the answer."[7] Like so many predictions made about the Vietnam War, Eisenhower's proved to be hopelessly wrong.

Chapter 2

The United States Takes Charge

As France's power and influence in Vietnam lessened, the United States took steps to increase its own presence. In October 1955, the Americans sent economic and military aid directly to South Vietnam, not France. Though this move infuriated the French government, most American officials believed further aid to their old ally was a waste of money, especially when France began to pull out of Vietnam. In April 1956, only fifteen thousand French troops remained in Vietnam, and by September all were gone.

In the absence of the French, the United States sent increasing numbers of its own armed forces to Vietnam. But this was nothing really new; U.S. military personnel had been involved in anti-Communist actions in Vietnam for years. Even before the Geneva Conference had ended, specially trained American agents under the command of Colonel Edward G. Lansdale infiltrated Hanoi and carried out various undercover acts intended to disturb the everyday life of the North Vietnamese. Among other things, the agents contaminated the fuel tanks of city buses in Hanoi to disrupt transportation. They also spread rumors and distributed leaflets that claimed Communists planned to persecute Catholics. These stories helped to cause nearly 1 million Catholics to flee to the South. Anti-Communist infiltrators also played on the fears of superstitious rural people of North Vietnam by hiring astrologers who predicted a bad future for Ho Chi Minh and a promising one for Ngo Dinh Diem, a fervent anti-Communist born in Central Vietnam who had returned from exile in the United States to serve as prime minister for Bao Dai in South Vietnam.

To the relief of the United States, Diem refused to hold the 1956 national elections as called for by the Geneva Conference. Diem argued that the Geneva agreement was mainly between France and North Vietnam. Because the government of South

Ngo Dinh Diem, the leader of South Vietnam during the early years of the Vietnam War, was supported by the U.S. because of his anti-Communist stance.

South Vietnam the chance to choose between himself and former emperor Bao Dai for president. Amid accusations of election fraud, Diem emerged victorious with a suspiciously high 98 percent of the vote and declared himself president of a new, independent government called the Republic of Vietnam.

Though these bold actions strengthened Diem's position, the Eisenhower administration privately doubted his ability to lead South Vietnam. Not only did Diem face hostility from Communists in the North and rebellion from Communist rebels in the South, he also had to contend with armed opposition from a powerful group of gangsters in Saigon called the Binh Xuyen. American observers were also troubled by the quality of men within Diem's own government. Many of his handpicked officials were corrupt. They used public funds for their own purposes and accepted bribes.

Nor did Americans have much confidence in the Army of South Vietnam (ARVN). Many U.S. military advisers and officials considered the ARVN ill equipped, undisciplined, and unmotivated. In addition, many of the ARVN's own troops had fought alongside the French against Communist troops and were now uncertain of

Vietnam did not officially agree to the terms, he said, it was not bound to observe them. Diem did agree, however, to set up a different election that offered the voters of

The U.S. had little confidence in the Army of South Vietnam (ARVN) and questioned the loyalty, preparation, discipline, and motivation of its soldiers.

their loyalty to the new Republic of Vietnam that was replacing French rule.

Diem had also angered many of his countrymen. Among other unpopular measures, he outlawed the centuries-old custom practiced by rural people of electing village councils. Instead, Diem appointed to these important positions his own men, who generally knew nothing about the communities they represented.

In addition, he failed to carry out meaningful land reform—an important issue in a country of peasants where most of the land was owned by less that 20 percent of the population. Instead he infuriated many

South Vietnamese peasants with his "strategic hamlet" program in 1959. Under the plan, Diem's troops removed thousands of South Vietnamese villagers from their ancestral lands and placed them in new, fortified, fenced communities. Though the program was meant to protect villagers from the Viet Minh—or Viet Cong (Vietnamese slang for Communists), as Diem now called them—thousands of peasants nonetheless resented the relocation effort and the cramped, inhospitable conditions they were forced to live in.

Finally, unchecked religious bigotry within the Diem regime created social unrest within South Vietnam. This prejudice was centuries old. Many of Vietnam's past emperors disliked Buddhism—a religion imported from India—and preferred Confucianism, a belief system from China that emphasized social order and obedience to a ruler. The French gave the religious bias against Buddhism a new twist when they took over Vietnam and introduced Catholicism as the one true religion. A practicing catholic, Diem had little sympathy for Buddhists. As president, he gave key government positions to fellow Christians and none to Buddhists. Although Catholics made up only 10 percent of the population, they controlled most of the government. Diem also chose his brother Ngo Dinh Nhu, to head the secret police—a position that Nhu often used to punish political enemies, including thousands of Buddhists. Diem's actions angered many South Vietnamese and provoked intense

opposition from the Communists. When he refused to hold the 1956 elections, the Viet Minh launched a campaign to overthrow him and reunify Vietnam under the Communist principles practiced in North Vietnam. They were not alone. Behind the scenes, the government of North Vietnam provided the rebels with materiel, money, and military intelligence.

The Transformation of North Vietnam

Opposition to Diem, however, did not mean leaders in North Vietnam were any less brutal with their own people. In many ways life was even worse for thousands of North Vietnamese. To transform North Vietnam into a Communist regime, Ho Chi Minh and his fellow Communists imposed a brutal dictatorship upon the people. Armed commandos tolerated no dissent and murdered thousands of opponents. The Communists took over businesses and factories and forced the entire population of Vietnam to accept a political and economic system that most played no role in creating or running. Unlike Diem, Ho did redistribute land more equally to the landless, but his men all too often used brutality to carry out this reform. Communist soldiers may have killed or deported as many as six thousand North Vietnamese farmers who refused to cooperate with the government's demand to confiscate their land and share with others. But Ho and his advisers decided to put off many other social and economic reforms they had

A North Vietnamese Soldier's Diary

Robert Goldston's *The Vietnamese Revolution* contains these ten "disciplinary rules for military security" taken from a diary begun in 1961 by Do Luc, a North Vietnamese soldier who was killed in the same year.

1. Do not disclose army secrets. Do not be curious about your own responsibilities and duties.

2. Do not discuss the duties you must carry out.

3. You must respect absolutely the regulations which protect documents during your activities. . . .

4. Keep secret our method of hiding weapons.

5. Do not take the liberty of listening to enemy broadcasts or reading their newspapers or documents. Do not spread false rumors.

6. Do not have relations with any organization with evil segments of the population which are harmful to the revolution.

7. Do not take your family or relatives or friends to military campsites.

8. Keep order and security among the populations as well as among yourselves.

9. Do not cease to carry out self-criticism or being vigilant, and continue your training.

10. Implement seriously these ten rules, mentally as well as in deeds.

In January 1959, the new leaders of North Vietnam announced official support of the Communist uprising in the South. In September 1960, they went even further by publicly voicing their intention of overthrowing Diem's government. Three months later, the Viet Cong created the National Liberation Front (the NLF) to carry out this goal. Soon, armed troops from the NLF infiltrated the countryside of South Vietnam and launched a campaign of death and terror. Using the same hit-and-run tactics they had once employed against the French, Communist troops now murdered teachers, social workers, and medical helpers in the villages of South Vietnam to convince others that they should submit to the Communist regime.

Dissent Grows in South Vietnam

When the ARVN appeared incapable of protecting the villagers from these brutal attacks, Diem asked for help from the United States. In response, President Eisenhower sent members of the U.S. Army Special Forces to train South Vietnamese soldiers in the art of secret military operations. But this instruction had little effect; the Communist guerrillas continued to win the hearts and minds of rural villagers in South Vietnam who were fed up with the policies of their own government.

Dissatisfaction with Diem intensified throughout Vietnam. In April 1960, eighteen prominent South Vietnamese citizens signed their names to a proclamation that criticized his government. Other dissidents

planned until after they had accomplished their main political goal—the reunification of Vietnam under Communist control.

took more violent measures. Some tried to kill Diem and his brother on several occasions. Though these attempts failed, they helped convince many American observers that Diem was fast losing the support of his own people.

A New President Takes Charge

In January 1961, a new president took office in the United States—John Kennedy, formerly a senator from Massachusetts.

Kennedy faced many foreign policy problems. Among them was ongoing trouble in the Caribbean island country of Cuba. In 1959, during the Eisenhower administration, a revolutionary named Fidel Castro had violently seized power in Cuba and installed a Communist dictatorship. Many Cubans fled to the United States to avoid his brutal rule and put together an army of exiles determined to overthrow him.

Cuban American leaders expected Kennedy to honor a pledge Eisenhower made to provide American aircraft to support the invading troops of Cuba. But Kennedy failed to provide adequate military help. Without it, the invasion ended in disaster. Many Cuban Americans were killed, wounded, or imprisoned. This incident, known as the Bay of Pigs invasion, caused bitterness toward Kennedy in the Cuban American community for decades.

Stung by the resulting criticism that he was "soft on Communism," Kennedy also had to contend with the rising opposition to Diem's rule and the growing menace of Communism in South Vietnam. In the early days

Soon after entering office in 1961, President John Kennedy was criticized for being soft on Communism.

of his term, the new president continued Eisenhower's policy of sending military instructors to South Vietnam to support the ARVN. But as conditions worsened in Vietnam, U.S. officials agonized over what they should do next. Many, along with Kennedy, viewed the conflict as a civil war that should be of limited concern to the United States. Others within his administration disagreed. Like many of their predecessors, they saw the American effort in Vietnam as an important part of a worldwide struggle against the expansion of Communism. As the leader of the free world, they argued, the United States had a duty to protect an ally that was struggling against aggression.

In 1961, Diem asked for more U.S. assistance, saying, "The level of their [the Communists] attacks is already such that our forces are stretched to their utmost."[8] In response, Kennedy sent Vice President Lyndon Johnson and special military adviser General Maxwell Taylor to South Vietnam to make a personal survey of the situation there. Both men recommended sending men and military supplies to help Diem's army.

Kennedy was willing to help, but he was wary of sending in combat troops. Instead, he took measures to enhance the fighting ability of the ARVN. Among other steps, the new president sent four hundred Special Forces soldiers—the U.S. Army's specially trained commandos—along with one hundred military advisers to train the ARVN. The Kennedy administration also agreed to pay for a thirty-thousand-man increase in the ARVN and supply the South Vietnamese with helicopters and armored personnel carriers.

In response to Diem's plea for assistance, the Kennedy administration sent helicopters (below), armored personnel carriers, Special Forces soldiers, and military advisers.

Torturing the Enemy

In his book, *Vietnam: A History*, Stanley Karnow, a journalist who covered much of the Vietnam War, gives this eyewitness report of the torture a suspected Viet Minh prisoner received at the hands of a so-called South Vietnamese security committee:

> I myself watched an interrogation in a Mekong delta town on a blistering hot day in the late 1950s. Soldiers had brought in a lean youth in black cotton pajamas who looked like any peasant. He squatted impassively, as if stoically awaiting a fate he could not avoid. The soldiers wired his fingers to a field telephone, then cranked it as an officer spoke with surprising gentleness to the youth, trying to extract either information or a confession. The youth gritted his teeth, his facial muscles taut as the electricity coursed through his body, and he finally blurted out a few words, perhaps only to stop the ordeal.
>
> I was relieved when he talked, but the officer refused to tell me what he had said, nor where the youth was being taken as the soldiers led him away. He may have been re-

leased. He may have been executed. He may have been banished to Poulo Condore, the island prison formerly used by the French to cage Vietnamese nationalists. I also knew that Diem's police frequently shot prisoners—reporting that they had been killed attempting to escape.

The South Vietnamese often tortured Viet Minh prisoners to obtain information or seek revenge.

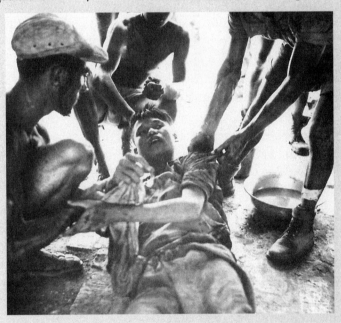

By the end of the year 3,164 Americans were stationed in Vietnam. A year later that number more than tripled. Though some of these troops secretly carried out sabotage missions, the U.S. government publicly claimed all were military advisers, not combat troops.

Diem Loses Support

Meanwhile, several events in South Vietnam further dissolved public support for Diem. In the wake of several assassination attempts on his brother and himself, Diem cracked down on all dissenters and protesters against his regime. His troops rounded up thousands of political opponents and imprisoned them. They also persecuted Buddhists everywhere. Many of Diem's opponents were never seen again. This brutal repression, however, did little to stop protests against Diem and his government. Instead, it ignited widespread hatred and resistance to his rule. The war against the Communists was also going badly for Diem. South Vietnamese everywhere were increasingly dismayed that he seemed unable to prevent the guerrilla warfare.

Another blow to his prestige came on January 2, 1963. Despite massive military aid and training from the United States, many ARVN soldiers lost their nerve in combat at Ap Bac hamlet, located forty miles from Saigon, and allowed a great number of enemy troops they had encircled to escape. This battlefield failure gave the Viet Cong a psychological boost. It also caused many American military planners to give up on Diem's regime.

More trouble arose on May 8 when Buddhists gathered in Hue to celebrate the 2,527th birthday of Buddha, the founder of Buddhism. Conditions in the ancient city were tense from the start because Major Dang Xi, a Catholic official in Diem's government, put into effect an old decree that banned the display of the multicolored Buddhist flags during the festivities. Buddhists were offended by this ban, especially since Xi had encouraged Catholics to exhibit their blue-and-white banners during a Catholic religious celebration only a week before.

When thousands of Buddhists peacefully gathered in the streets to protest the ban, ARVN soldiers arrived to disperse them. As tension mounted, gunshots rang out and caused a stampede. When the melee subsided, a woman and eight children lay dead, either trampled or shot to death.

Diem tried in vain to blame the deaths on the Viet Cong. But across South Vietnam angry Buddhists staged protests and placed responsibility for the killings on the government. They also condemned the United States for backing Diem and his regime. As one Buddhist leader and monk, Tri Quang, told a U.S. official in Saigon: "The United States must either make Diem reform or get rid of him. If not the situation will degenerate, and you worthy gentlemen will suffer most. You are responsible for the present trouble because you back Diem and his government of ignoramuses."[9]

Buddhist outrage over the killings soon took a new and gruesome form. On the morning of June 11, 1963, Quang Duc, a sixty-three-year-old Buddhist monk, sat down on the pavement of a busy street in Saigon. Suddenly, a younger monk doused him with gasoline. Then the older man lit a match. Astonished onlookers fell to the ground in reverence as Quang Duc went up in flames. Supporters later explained that the old monk intended his self-immolation to encourage Diem to show respect and tolerance for all religions.

Relations between Buddhists and Catholics worsened when other monks in

Self-Sacrifice

In Saigon on the morning of June 11, 1963, Associated Press correspondent Malcolm Browne witnessed the self-immolation of Quang Duc, the first of many Buddhists to burn himself alive to protest the repression of the South Vietnamese government. The account appears in *The Eyewitness History of the Vietnam War: 1961–1975*, written by Vietnam War correspondent George Esper.

[After a Buddhist monk doused Quang Duc with gasoline] I could see Quang Duc move his hands slightly in his lap striking a match. In a flash, he was sitting in the center of a column of flame, which engulfed his entire body. A wail of horror rose from the monks and nuns, many of whom prostrated themselves in the direction of the flames.

From time to time, a light breeze pulled the flames away from Quang Duc's face. His eyes were closed, but his features were twisted in apparent pain. He remained upright, his hands folded in his lap, for nearly ten minutes as the flesh burned from his head and body. The reek of gasoline smoke and burning flesh hung over the intersection like a pall.

Finally, Quang Duc fell backwards, his blackened legs kicking convulsively for a minute or so. Then he was still, and the flames gradually subsided.

In protest against the inhumanity and bloodshed of the war, some Buddhist monks set themselves aflame.

Vietnam also set themselves on fire. Madame Ngo Dinh Nhu, the outspoken wife of one of Diem's brothers, added to the crisis when she ridiculed the burnings. "All the Buddhists have done for this country is to barbecue a monk,"[10] she said.

Televised images of the burnings shocked viewers around the world and prompted international condemnation of the Diem government. American officials too were unnerved by the spectacle and tried without success to pressure Diem to call off his crackdown on the Buddhists. By now many condemned Diem's dictatorial methods and viewed them as an embarrassment. How could the United States insist it was supporting democracy in South Vietnam when Diem's troops were so oblivious to human rights? they asked.

In late August, disapproval of Diem intensified when he declared martial law in South Vietnam and ordered a military crackdown on Communist activists. Once again his troops also targeted Buddhists. In dozens of cities, they smashed pagodas and Buddhist shrines and arrested monks and thousands of supporters. They also killed many Buddhists.

Though the raids momentarily halted the Buddhist uprisings, they infuriated many South Vietnamese and millions of Americans. Kennedy, in response to mounting public outrage over the crackdown, temporarily halted all economic and military aid to South Vietnam on October 2, 1963.

The Plot to Oust Diem

Kennedy's rebuke convinced many South Vietnamese officials that the Americans no longer had faith in Diem. Among them were several military officers belonging to a secret group who wished to topple the high-handed leader. Until now the conspirators had hesitated to act because they were unsure how the Americans would react to a military coup. Some generals feared that U.S. military aid would be cut off if Diem were ousted.

As support for Diem collapsed, social unrest mounted in South Vietnam. Attacks on Buddhist dissidents continued. Both Madame Nhu and her husband openly denounced U.S. officials and American journalists for their criticism of government attacks against Buddhists. Meanwhile, the Viet Cong took advantage of the chaos and escalated their attacks against villages in the countryside.

The continuing widespread disorder threatened to undermine American foreign policy. Controversy over Diem also raged within the Kennedy administration. Many presidential advisers believed the United States should back the conspirators and bring new leadership to South Vietnam. Others thought Madame Nhu and her husband, not Diem himself, needed to be removed. Remembering the Bay of Pigs fiasco, some officials worried that an unsuccessful coup could once again embarrass the president. A few advisers, including top military adviser, General Paul Harkins, argued Diem was South Vietnam's legitimate ruler and the United States had no right to decide his fate. Kennedy's younger brother, Robert, who served as the nation's attorney general, wondered if any government in South Vietnam could permanently resist Communism. Perhaps, he argued, "Now was the time to get out of Vietnam entirely."[11]

In the end, Henry Cabot Lodge, the U.S. ambassador to South Vietnam, conveyed the final American position to the conspirators in Vietnam: The United States would not openly support a coup, nor would it prevent one. Despite the ambiguity of the statement, the plotters interpreted it as an invitation for them to act. As the rebel generals planned their coup, high officials in the Kennedy administration grew jittery and ordered Lodge to urge the conspirators to postpone their coup.

But Lodge, a harsh critic of Diem, never delivered this message. At 4 A.M. on November 2, rebels opened fire on the presidential palace in Saigon. At first, Diem and his brother believed the attack was the first phase of a phony coup, designed by Nhu to confuse the real conspirators. All too soon they realized they were wrong. The false coup never occurred.

Two and a half hours after the first shots were fired, palace guards surrendered as Diem and his brother escaped through a secret passageway. They spent several hours in a futile attempt to raise a fighting force to oppose the military coup. Finally, at about 9 A.M., they gave up and surrendered to the conspirators. Though Diem and Nhu received promises of safe passage out of Vietnam, ARVN soldiers shot and stabbed them as they were escorted from Saigon.

Kennedy was shocked when he heard the news of Diem's death. Worried that the killings might ignite social disorder, the president ordered the American Seventh Fleet in the South China Sea to head for Vietnam to protect Americans stationed there in case rioting occurred. But the mood in South Vietnam was euphoric. Cheering people clogged the streets of Saigon and other cities. Ambassador Lodge congratulated the generals for their successful coup.

Soon, however, even those who favored the coup realized that Diem's death did nothing to improve the situation in South Vietnam. Diem may have been

Reluctance to Bring Down an Ally

As President Diem's generals plotted to overthrow him in the fall of 1963, U.S. officials were divided about whether to support the coup. In this cablegram to General Maxwell Taylor, who served as chairman of the Joint Chiefs of Staff and later as ambassador to South Vietnam, excerpted from Quadrangle Books's edition of *The Pentagon Papers,* General Paul Harkins, the head of a military advisory mission to South Vietnam, makes it clear he has misgivings about the conspiracy.

I am not a Diem man per se. I certainly see the faults in his character. I am here to back 14 million SVN [South Vietnamese] people in their fight against Communism and it just happens that Diem is their leader at this time. Most of the Generals I have talked to agree they can go along with Diem, all say it's the Nhu family they are opposed to. . . .

After all, rightly or wrongly, we have backed Diem for eight long hard years. To me it seems incongruous now to get him down, kick him around, and get rid of him. The U.S. has been his mother superior and father confessor since he's been in office and he has leaned on us heavily.

Leaders of other under-developed countries will take a dim view of our assistance if they too were led to believe the same fate lies in store for them.

flawed, but now there was no other person powerful enough to take his place. With South Vietnam still in chaos, many U.S. officials concluded it was time to win the war or get out.

For the moment, however, Kennedy ordered no withdrawal of U.S. advisers from South Vietnam. But he may have had serious plans to disengage Americans from Vietnam after the presidential election in 1964. At a press conference the day before the coup, Kennedy provided a hint of what he may have had in mind: "Now, that is our object, to bring Americans home. Permit the South Vietnamese to maintain themselves as a free and independent country, and permit democratic forces within the country to operate."[12]

Kennedy was never able to implement these plans. Three weeks after his speech, he lay dead in Dallas, the victim of an assassin's bullets. Suddenly, both South Vietnam and its most important ally had lost their most experienced leaders. In this vacuum of leadership, the Viet Cong waged war with renewed vigor.

Chapter 3

Johnson's War

During the following months, the government of South Vietnam became dangerously unstable. All too soon, the military coup that seized power proved itself inept and corrupt. Its leaders managed to stay in power for only a few months. Afterward, one corrupt, dictatorial government after another rose and fell from power. All of them undermined American claims that U.S. forces helped to support democratically elected officials in South Vietnam. Fears ran high in Washington that eventually power in South Vietnam would fall into the hands of politicians who would compromise with the Communists and undercut American political intentions.

Adding to this sense of alarm were ever-increasing Communist attacks against South Vietnamese and American troops. Worse yet, these assaults were also becoming

deadlier because many Communist soldiers now carried new Soviet weapons, such as the Russian-made Kalashnikov AK-47—an assault rifle capable of firing ten

New Soviet weapons, such as the Kalashnikov AK-47 rifle (pictured here with its designer, Mikhail Kalashnikov), gave the Viet Cong an advantage over the ARVN.

rounds per second. These weapons gave the Viet Cong superior fire power over many ARVN troops, who still used older American-made M1 carbine rifles.

Communist insurgents also continued to seize more and more territory in South Vietnam. In addition, they were winning the allegiance of increasing numbers of South Vietnamese villagers who had grown wary of their own government and the Americans.

Troubling Options

How to respond to the growing crisis in Vietnam fell to America's new president, Lyndon Johnson—Kennedy's vice president, who had been sworn into the presidency within hours after the assassination. Johnson was very different from the urbane, polished, Boston-bred Kennedy. A tall, lanky, engaging man from rural Texas, Johnson spoke with a folksy drawl and often exhibited personal habits and traits that struck many as offensive and vulgar. But he was also an intelligent, knowledgeable, and shrewd leader who had honed powerful skills of persuasion and deal making during his many years as a representative and senator in the U.S. Congress.

Despite many political and philosophical differences with Kennedy, Johnson shared Kennedy's view that the United States was the only free country in the world powerful enough to put down a global threat to world peace. Since he had inherited the presidency, Johnson believed his immediate duty was to finish out Kennedy's

term of office by following his predecessor's policies as much as possible. For the moment, he continued Kennedy's policy of providing training and logistical support to the ARVN. But in the summer of 1964, an event took place off the Vietnam coast that caused Johnson to change his policy and pave the way for a much bigger war.

The Gulf of Tonkin Incident

On July 30, 1964, two South Vietnamese gunboats opened fire against an enemy radar installation on Hon Me, an island near the northern coast of North Vietnam. Two other boats, meanwhile, attacked one of North Vietnam's busiest ports on the island of Hon Ngu. The USS *Maddox*, an American destroyer, cruised eleven miles off the coast of North Vietnam and monitored all the radio dispatches that took place during the attack. North Vietnam officials later learned of the *Maddox*'s presence and claimed the American ship violated a twelve-mile zone they considered territorial waters. They also officially complained to the International Control Commission, the multinational organization set up by the Geneva Conference to monitor the 1954 agreement.

Despite these protests, American officials ordered the *Maddox* to remain in the area. On August 2 the destroyer was headed for the open sea when three North Vietnamese torpedo boats pursued it and fired torpedoes. With the help of needle-nosed Crusader fighter-bomber jets sent from the USS *Ticonderoga*, an aircraft car-

Within hours of Kennedy's assassination, Lyndon Johnson was sworn into the presidency. He would continue to support the ARVN as Kennedy had done.

rier in the region, the crew of the *Maddox* returned fire at the torpedo boats and within twenty minutes sank one and disabled the other two. No American was hurt in the skirmish. Only one bullet managed to hit the *Maddox*, and all torpedoes missed their targets.

Now American officials expressed outrage. They insisted the U.S. ships were in international waters and presented no threat to the North Vietnamese. Soon U.S.

combat troops went on alert, and extra U.S. fighter-bombers flew to American bases located in South Vietnam and neighboring Thailand. Instead of pulling the *Maddox* out of harm's way, Johnson ordered another destroyer, the USS *C. Turner*

Joy, to join the *Maddox.* Now two American ships cruised off the coast of Vietnam to demonstrate a right to sail these waters. "The *Maddox* and the *Turner Joy* were effectively being used to bait the Communists,"[13] writes author Stanley Karnow.

Tensions ran high on both American ships as sailors prepared for more attacks. At eight o'clock that night both crews went on full alert when personnel aboard the *Maddox* believed they had intercepted Communist radio messages and troubling radar signals that indicated an attack was imminent.

All at once tense Americans opened fire into the night in all directions. When their panic subsided, however, no hostile craft was visible. Nor had anyone aboard either American ship heard any hostile gunfire, though some sailors reported sightings of approaching boats and torpedoes in the darkness. "I saw, with my own eyes, five or more high-speed contacts approaching on the surface-search radar," reported Ensign John Leeman, who stood watch on the bridge at 8 P.M. "I saw this."[14] But American pilots who circled above the ships in planes dispatched from nearby aircraft carriers reported no sign of the North Vietnamese.

The USS C. Turner Joy *was sent to join the USS* Maddox *off the coast of North Vietnam to demonstrate America's right to sail in those waters.*

Confused and frightened, the crews of both ships wondered exactly what had happened. John J. Herrick, the captain of the *Maddox*, reported the incident to his superiors in Washington, along with his doubts that there had been an enemy attack against the American ships: "Review of action makes many reported contacts and torpedoes fired appear doubtful. Freak weather effects and overeager sonarmen may have accounted for many reports. No actual visual sighting by *Maddox*. Suggest complete evaluation before any further action."[15]

Despite Herrick's uncertainty, the Johnson administration insisted that a hostile strike had taken place that demanded swift retaliation from the United States. On the evening of August 4, Johnson appeared on television and solemnly spoke to the American people: "Repeated acts of violence against the armed forces of the United States must be met not only with alert defense, but with positive reply. That reply is being given as I speak to you tonight."[16] As the president spoke, U.S. naval bombers pounded sixty-four targets, including patrol bases and oil storage depots in North Vietnam.

Even though Johnson publicly asserted that the *Maddox* had been threatened, he may have suspected that evidence for the alleged attacks was hard to find. "Hell, those dumb stupid sailors were just shooting at flying fish,"[17] the president later told an aide. But Johnson and his staff kept their doubts private. The next day the president convinced the U.S. Congress that the American

Johnson Responds to an Uncertain Threat

Carl Albert, a majority leader of the House of Representatives from 1962 to 1971, recalls observing President Johnson respond to news that North Vietnamese had attacked U.S. ships. This passage appears in *American History: Reconstruction Through the Present*, edited by Robert James Maddox.

My years in Congress saw the Vietnam War from its very inception to its very end. I was in the Oval Office with President Johnson in August 1964 right after the Tonkin Gulf incident happened. The President and I were in his office alone. I was Majority Leader of the House of Representatives at the time. The phone rang, and he answered it.

I heard the President say that he wanted immediate retaliation, that he wanted the retaliation to be extensive, that he wanted the Air Force to do more than simply sink the patrol boats that were involved in the affair. He wanted all the facilities used by the North Vietnamese for the purpose of launching the attack destroyed and rendered unfit for further such operations. The next day the President sent to the Congress a resolution that was known as the Tonkin Gulf Resolution, asking for authority to wage the attack that he had talked about on the telephone. There was no opposition to the resolution in the House of Representatives. In fact, the vote was unanimous. Only two United States senators voted against it when the resolution reached that body. One was Sen. Wayne Morse of Oregon: the other was Sen. Ernest Gruening of Alaska. Incidentally, both of these senators were defeated in the next election by the people of their states.

ships had been attacked. In response, the lawmakers quickly passed a strongly worded piece of legislation called the "Gulf of Tonkin Resolution." This resolution gave Johnson the authority to wage war in Southeast Asia as necessary to protect American personnel. According to a Johnson aide the resolution was "the functional equivalent of a declaration of war." [18]

The Power to Make War

The resolution gave Johnson a new and controversial power. Like all presidents before him, Johnson was bound by the U.S. Constitution. Though this document gives the president of the United States the right to be commander in chief of the nation's armed forces, it does not allow him to declare war. Only Congress has this right.

But the 1964 Gulf of Tonkin Resolution gave the president the authority to use military force without a full congressional declaration of war. At the time, however, few Americans were upset by what Congress had done. As a result, Johnson faced almost no organized opposition as he steered his country into the longest war in its history without a serious discussion in Congress over whether this action was in the country's best interest.

Johnson also received a political boost from his decisive actions. At the moment, a presidential campaign was underway. Johnson faced a tough republican opponent—Barry Goldwater, a conservative senator from Arizona who argued that Johnson was too weak a leader to conduct

a war in Vietnam. But Goldwater's accusation seemed hollow in light of the air strikes Johnson had ordered on North Vietnam. At the same time, however, Johnson also campaigned that he favored peace in Vietnam and was not a warmonger like his opponent. Although Johnson was laying the groundwork for an escalation of the war, his public words told a different story: "We are not about to send American boys nine or ten thousand miles away from home to do what Asian boys ought to be doing for themselves." [19]

By maintaining this twin public image as a man of peace and a man of military action, Johnson was elected president in November 1964. Convinced he had a mandate from the American people, he felt freed from Kennedy's policies. Now he could follow his own agenda.

Charting His Own Way

Johnson also believed his election victory gave him authority to carry out many new ideas. Among them was his "Great Society" project. It was a massive domestic undertaking designed to use the power and resources of the federal government to help poor and underprivileged Americans on a scale that overshadowed anything ever before attempted in the nation's history.

Johnson soon realized the Vietnam War would interfere with this effort. The nation did not have the time and resources to wage war and solve massive social and economic problems at the same time. As Johnson once told biographer Doris Kearns:

I knew from the start that I was bound to be crucified either way I moved. If I left the woman I really loved—the Great Society—in order to get involved with that . . . war on the other side of the world, then I would lose everything at home. All my programs. All my hopes to feed the hungry and shelter the homeless. All my dreams to provide education and medical care to the browns and the blacks and the lame and the poor. But if I left that war and let the Communists take over South Vietnam, then I would be seen as a coward and my nation would be seen as an appeaser and we would both find it impossible to accomplish anything for anybody anywhere on the entire globe.[20]

Frustrated by these conflicting demands, Johnson wavered and rejected pleas from advisers to begin a massive bombing campaign to check Communist advances. He held fast to this position even after a Communist attack on an American air force base in Bien Hoa on November 1, 1964, killed five Americans and two Vietnamese and injured nearly a hundred others. The raid also destroyed six B-57 light bombers and damaged over twenty other aircraft. On Christmas Eve, Communists struck again with a bombing attack on a Saigon hotel for American officers. The attack killed two and wounded ninety-eight.

Johnson's advisers increased their calls for retaliation. On January 27, 1965, the head of the national security staff, McGeorge Bundy, sent the president a memo he had written with Robert McNamara, the secretary of defense, that warned of a disaster in South Vietnam unless America changed course. The two stated, "We agree . . . the time has come for harder choices."[21] Johnson's aides believed the president had two options: he could either pull the United States out of Vietnam or dramatically increase its military involvement to defeat the Communists. But to

The Communists bombed a Saigon hotel housing American officers on Christmas Eve, 1964.

maintain a middle course as the administration was doing, they argued, invited certain calamity.

Still Johnson hesitated. He believed escalation was dangerous. For one thing, it could lengthen the war and cost more American lives. It might also provoke North Vietnam's allies, China and the Soviet Union, to join the war against the United States, possibly igniting a third world war. Finally, Johnson also believed a major military push would be expensive and divert energy, resources, manpower, and leadership away from his Great Society.

Still postponing a final decision, he asked Bundy to visit Vietnam for a closer look at the situation. Ten days later, the Viet Cong raided an American installation in the city of Pleiku and killed nine U.S. soldiers. This event infuriated Johnson. "We have kept our gun over the mantel and our shells in the cupboard for a long time now," he told his aides. "And what was the result? They are killing our men while they sleep in the night."[22]

The next day Bundy returned from his trip and presented his findings: Unless the United States stepped up its involvement, the report said, the fall of South Vietnam was certain. In addition, he declared, "The international prestige of the United States and a substantial part of our influence are directly at risk in Vietnam."[23]

But Johnson had already made a decision. On February 7 he ordered retaliatory air strikes against selected targets in North Vietnam. Among them was the Ho Chi Minh Trail—a long pathway used by Communists in the North to supply the Viet Cong in the South. On March 2 the president intensified the attacks when he ordered a continuous bombing campaign that would continue for three years. Known as "Operation Rolling Thunder," it targeted enemy bases, railroad yards, and other military sites. That day 160 U.S. warplanes bombed North Vietnam. Johnson hoped this display of American military power would achieve several objectives. Above all else he wanted to force the Communists to the bargaining table and boost morale among the South Vietnamese people. He also wanted to demonstrate to the international community his determination to use military force when necessary to contain the spread of Communism

The Limits of Bombing

Many American war planners soon realized air power alone could not stem the tide of Communist aggression in South Vietnam. Nor could it dampen the fighting spirit of the Communists. No matter how much damage American bombs inflicted, the people of North Vietnam quickly rebuilt their supply trails, buildings, homes, and military units and resumed their relentless assault in the South. The bombing also failed to boost morale among ARVN troops, as Johnson had hoped. Instead, the desertion rate among the South Vietnamese army soared.

Faced with these results, Johnson agreed with his advisers that bombing

An American bomber releases its weapons during Operation Rolling Thunder.

alone was not enough. The time had come to send in combat troops. On March 10, 1965, the president ordered fifteen-hundred marines to the American air base in Da Nang, with more on the way. Six weeks later, fifty-thousand American troops were stationed in South Vietnam.

Though they were combat ready, the troops were under orders to use deadly force only to protect American bases. Soon, however, new orders arrived that gave them permission to go on military patrols to protect ARVN units. In June, they learned they could kill Communist soldiers without any South Vietnamese being present.

As the months passed, their numbers grew. By the end of 1965, 184,000 American troops were stationed in Vietnam. By

Johnson's Agony

In her book *Lyndon Johnson and the American Dream,* biographer Doris Kearns relates the words of anguish President Lyndon Johnson revealed to her during an interview concerning his decision to order bombing raids on North Vietnam.

In the dark at night, I would lay awake picturing my boys flying around North Vietnam, asking myself an endless series of questions. What if one of those targets you picked today triggers off Russia or China? What happens then? Or suppose one of my boys misses his mark when he's flying around Haiphong? Suppose one of his bombs falls on one of those Russian ships in the harbor? What happens then? Or sup-

pose the fog is too thick or the clouds are too high or the target too small and the bomb drops by mistake within the thirty-mile radius of Hanoi? . . .

I would then begin to picture myself lying on the battlefield in Da Nang. I could see an American plane circling above me in the sky. I felt safe. Then I heard a long, loud shot. The plane began to fall faster, faster, faster. I saw it hit the ground, and as soon as it burst into flames, I couldn't stand it any more. I knew that one of my boys must have been killed that night. I jumped out of bed, put on my robe, took my flashlight, and went into the Situation Room.

the end of 1966, their strength had grown to four-hundred thousand. This historic American military buildup in an Asian country took place without a declaration of war by the U.S. Congress. Only later did critics express alarm over what had happened. Historian Doris Kearns observes, "The movement from bombs to troops without the approval, discussion, or even the awareness of Congress was a stunning revelation of changes in the balance of power between the institu-

tion of American government and how far we had come from the original understanding"[24] of the constitution concerning the power to wage war.

Johnson expanded the Vietnam War more than any president before him and tried almost single-handedly to run it. "They can't even bomb an outhouse without my approval,"[25] he once said. Small wonder critics soon tagged the conflict "Johnson's War."

Chapter 4

A Different Kind of War

The American military buildup changed the face of South Vietnam. Billions of dollars flowed into the country as U.S. military bases, airfields, helicopter pads, hospitals, stores, and recreation centers sprang up. Many private American businesses and companies also set up operations either to aid the American war effort or to provide services for American personnel. Army engineers and private contractors built bridges and roads and dug deep-sea ports along South Vietnam's east coast. The Americans also set up a vast communication system of cables and radio networks that linked U.S. installations with Washington, D.C., and other command centers worldwide.

Thousands of South Vietnamese prospered from these American boomtowns. A multitude of small restaurants, ice cream parlors, shops, and nightclubs that catered to young Americans appeared near the U.S. military installations and boosted the local economy. Black markets also flourished with merchandise and equipment stolen from American installations. Some vendors provided GIs with drugs and prostitutes.

The United States also saturated South Vietnam with weapons. Tanks, armored cars, jeeps, trucks, jet bombers, transport planes, helicopters, ships, patrol boats, and tons of small arms, M-16 rifles, rocket launchers, grenades and other explosives flooded into the country. With these weapons came foreign troops. In addition to the ever growing American fighting force, an estimated sixty thousand troops arrived from South Korea, Australia, Thailand, New Zealand, and the Philippines. Dozens of other countries sent noncombat personnel to help.

This huge buildup of troops and war-related materiel, coupled with orders authorizing combat against the Communists, meant a major conflict between the Americans and the Communists was just a matter

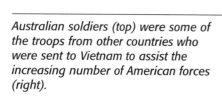

Australian soldiers (top) were some of the troops from other countries who were sent to Vietnam to assist the increasing number of American forces (right).

of time. Finally, that big clash came in November 1965 in the Ia Drang Valley in the Central Highlands of Vietnam.

The Battle of Ia Drang

Here, outnumbered seven to one, a battalion of the Seventh U.S. Cavalry battled North Vietnam regulars for the first time. The fighting was bloody and brutal for both sides. Men stabbed, shot, and blew each other up as American fighter-

bombers pounded the area with fire-bombs. For three days and two nights, the Americans held their ground. Finally, the North Vietnamese slipped away into Cambodia. Though U.S. troops lost 247 men, they killed more than 2,000 Communists.

General William Westmoreland, who now commanded U.S. forces in Vietnam, seized on enemy death tolls and proclaimed the battle of Ia Drang a U.S. victory. He, along with other American war planners, insisted that American troops had proved they could defeat the North Vietnamese on their own territory. Other officials were also quick to assert that the Americans were more competent than the South Vietnamese. William P. Bundy, then assistant secretary of state for East Asia, later wrote:

> Ia Drang . . . was a milestone. . . . It appeared to confirm the importance of . . . search-and-destroy [military missions] . . . and that American forces were especially effective in this role—a contrast that became more vivid when on November 28, a large South Vietnamese unit was ambushed and cut to pieces in the Michelin plantation northwest of Saigon.[26]

But many Americans who survived the madness at Ia Drang saw the situation much differently. One of them was Joseph L. Galloway, then a twenty-four-year-old civilian news correspondent and eyewitness at the battle. He writes:

> The U.S. too often lost, covered up or ignored the lessons of the Ia Drang— that the North Vietnamese soldier was brave and tough, that it would cost more American lives than anyone believed to defeat him and that it would be impossible to crush the North Vietnamese Army so long as it could escape into Cambodia. The first lesson came before the battle was over, when a 400-man battalion was cut to pieces after it

blundered into an ambush in a place called Landing Zone Albany.[27]

But American policy makers thought otherwise and decided to pursue the war. It was one they believed the United States could win.

The United States Takes the Lead

Before the Americans took charge of the ground war, South Vietnam appeared to be on the verge of collapse. But the newly

People Power

In a 1990 interview with *U.S. News & World Report,* General Vo Nguyen Giap reflected on the limits of American firepower in the battle of Ia Drang Valley.

The Americans didn't understand that we had our soldiers almost everywhere; that it was very hard to surprise us. When we heard the helicopters, we went on alert and prepared for battle wherever you landed. Being on the spot, everywhere, was the best mobility of all.

Even advanced weapons have weaknesses. We had our choice of weaknesses. You staged bombing raids in advance of your landings. During that time our soldiers were in their tunnels and bunkers and took very few casualties. When your armed helicopters came we were still in our shelters. Only when the helicopters brought your troops did we emerge, and only then did we start shooting. You Americans were very strong in modern weapons, but we were strong in something else. Our war was people's war, waged by the entire people. Our battlefield was everywhere, or nowhere, and the choice was ours.

arrived Americans reversed this trend— at least temporarily. Unlike the ARVN, they were well trained and possessed an arsenal of high-tech weaponry and well-equipped combat units. From Vietnam's marshes of the Mekong Delta to the mountain forests, U.S. troops used automatic weapons, machine guns, heavy artillery, howitzers, and rocket launchers. From the sky, huge B-52 bombers and Phantom jets unleashed cluster bombs, television-camera-guided air-to-surface missiles, and bombs containing napalm—

Unlike the ARVN, U.S. combat units were well equipped with automatic weapons, machine guns, heavy artillery, howitzers, and rocket launchers.

a jellied gas that splattered and then ignited.

American GIs used bulldozers to wipe out homes of villagers suspected of harboring Viet Cong. They also used an array of high-tech surveillance equipment such as infrared photography and ground-level radar to monitor movement of the Communists. Chemical warfare played a role too. American aircraft sprayed millions of gallons of Agent Orange, a powerful and controversial herbicide, across great swaths of Vietnamese countryside to destroy crops and vegetation that hid enemy troops and supply movements. U.S. pilots even tried, without much success, to seed clouds to create abnormal rainfall in North Vietnam.

The high-tech weapons of the United States soon forced the Communists to re-think how they waged war. Soon large scale assaults waged by the Viet Cong against American and ARVN ground forces in South Vietnam gave way to more smaller hit-and-run guerrilla tactics.

This shift in tactics troubled American military leaders. Unlike other American wars, this one had no clearly defined battle lines. Nor was the enemy readily identifiable, as Japanese and German troops had been in World War II. Often the Americans and their allies could not distinguish between the enemy and those they protected. Clad in straw hats and pajama-like clothing, Viet Cong saboteurs and assassins looked like most other villagers in South Vietnam. During the day, they were often courteous to Americans; at night they tried to kill them. Recalls Larry Phelps, a former U.S. Navy second class petty officer involved in combat-support helicopter duty, "Vietnam was a fantasy of unbelievable disorganization. Sometimes you wondered how incredible it was that you were here. How absurd."[28]

In such a confusing world, the superior firepower and technology of the Ameri-cans soon became less of an advantage. In addition, American soldiers, like the French before them, quickly learned the Communists were formidable warriors. What the Viet Cong lacked in advanced weaponry and technology they made up for in motivation and discipline. Mobile and quick, Communist troops seldom carried more than ten pounds on their backs while on maneuvers. In contrast, most American foot soldiers hauled fifty-pound loads. Unlike the Americans, the Viet Cong knew the terrain and could communicate with the villagers they tried to win over.

"I Did What I Was Told"

In this excerpt of an interview with the author, George Moore, a former Army Specialist and member of Charlie Rangers, recalls what he thought about being asked to wage war in Vietnam:

I was just like a bunch of the people. You're 19 or 20 years old, you're drafted, you go to boot camp and you do what you're told. Ninety-five percent of the guys didn't know what was right, what was wrong . . . they didn't call the shots, decide when to ambush, when not to, when not to go, when not to shoot. They did what they were told to. I was a PFC [private first class] and I did what I was told. I never asked my lieutenant, captain, or major, "Sir, do you think it's a good idea to waste these people?". . . I didn't ask if I was right or what was wrong. I don't think I had the right to. The higher-ups run the country. Out of the millions they picked from I was part of the crop.

Because their enemy proved so elusive, American military strategists decided to hunt them down with numerous "search-and-destroy" missions. These efforts followed a basic pattern. Once an enemy stronghold was detected, American bombers and heavy artillery pounded the site. Squadrons of heavily armed Huey helicopters—at times carrying hundreds of U.S. troops—sped to the site like huge, chattering, metal locusts. When they arrived, gunners opened fire with machine guns to rid the area of Communists and prepare a safe landing zone for American troops. Next, U.S. troops fanned out into the area and searched for Viet Cong to shoot. American officers often stressed the three Fs: "Find, fix, and finish."[29]

The Viet Cong were often prepared for such attacks. Now and then they assaulted American patrols deliberately to provoke a search-and-destroy mission. This gave them the chance to shoot down arriving helicopters. When American reinforcements chased them, the Viet Cong often suddenly disappeared into the jungles or secret underground tunnels. Hapless Americans who pursued them often ran into ambushes or detonated deadly land mines rigged with trip wires. Some fell into pits filled with bamboo stakes tipped with poison.

Assessing the Damage

Despite these hazards, the Americans persisted undaunted. Armed with superior firepower, U.S. troops, along with the ARVN, defeated North Vietnamese troops time and time again during the Johnson years. But they never seemed to get the upper hand over their adversary. At best, Americans could boast they had stood their ground. By the end of 1966, after fifty-one hundred American servicemen had been killed in Vietnam and thirty thousand wounded, U.S. officials still saw no end of the war. General Westmoreland decided it was time to abandon limited war tactics and switch to much larger ones.

On January 8, 1967, the Americans launched Operation Cedar Fall, the largest search-and-destroy mission yet. Its target was a Communist headquarters located near the village of Ben Suc, twenty miles northwest of Saigon. Arriving U.S. troops discovered the area was a Viet Cong stronghold teeming with Communist supporters. Americans bulldozed the village and blew up a maze of underground tunnels used by the Viet Cong. According to Lieutenant Colonel Joseph M. Kiernan, commander of the engineer battalion that carried out demolition of an area near the village:

> The place was so infested with tunnels that as my dozers would knock over the stumps of trees, the VC would pop out from behind the dozers. We captured about . . . six or eight VC one morning. After the civilians were taken from the town, we went through and methodically knocked down the homes . . . [T]unnels were through the whole area.[30]

An American soldier wounded in battle is taken to a hospital. Thirty thousand U.S. troops were wounded by the end of 1966.

In addition to destroying miles of tunnels and buildings, American GIs killed nearly 3,000 Communists. In contrast, the American death toll was reported to be 282.

An even bigger search-and-destroy operation code-named Operation Junction City took place the following month. On February 22, American fighter-bombers blasted an enemy base located northwest of Saigon near Cambodia; soon afterwards forty-five thousand U.S. troops swept into the area and killed three thousand Viet Cong.

Though these missions proved costly to the Viet Cong, they did not greatly alter the balance of power in Vietnam. By the end of 1967, the United States and ARVN controlled South Vietnam's major cities; but the Viet Cong commanded the countryside. Leaders on both sides realized that a stalemate had developed. Neither the Viet

Death Up Close

The Vietnam Reader, edited by Stewart O'Nan, contains this excerpt from Wallace Berry's *Bloods,* a collection of oral histories told by African Americans who served in Vietnam. In this passage, Private First Class Reginal "Malik" Edwards of Phoenix, Louisiana, a rifleman in the Ninth Regiment of the U.S. Marine Corps, recalls his first close-up look at a killing.

The first time I killed somebody up close was when we was tailing Charlie [Communists] on a patrol somewhere around Danang. It was night. I was real tired. At that time you had worked so hard during the day, been on so many different details, you were just bombed out.

I thought I saw this dog running. Because that white pajama top they wore at night just blend into that funny-colored night they had over there. All of a sudden, I realized that somebody's runnin'. And before I could say anything to him, he's almost ran up on me. There's nothing I can do but shoot. Somebody gets that close, you can't

wait to check their ID. He's gonna run into you or stop to shoot you. It's got to be one or the other. I shot him a bunch of times. I had a 20-round clip, and when he hit the ground, I had nothing. I had to reload. That's how many times he was shot.

Then the sergeant came over and took out the flashlight and said, ". . . This is . . . beautiful. This is . . . beautiful."

This guy was really out of it. He was like moanin'. I said, "Let me kill him." I couldn't stand the sound he was makin'. So I said, "Back off, man. Let me put this guy out of his misery." So I shot him again. In the head.

He had a grenade in his hand. I guess he was committing suicide. He was just runnin' up to us, pullin' a grenade kind of thing. I caught him just in time.

Everybody was comin' congratulatin' me, saying what a great thing it was. I'm trying to be cool, but I'm really freakin' out. So then I start walking away, and they told me I had to carry the body back to base camp. We had a real kill. We had one we could prove. We didn't have to make this one up.

So then I start draggin' this body by the feet. And his arm fell off. So I had to go back and get his arm. I had to stick it down his pants. It was a long haul.

And I started thinkin'. You think about how it feels, the weight. It was rainin'. You think about the mist and the smells the rain brings out. All of a sudden I realize this guy is a person, has got a family. All of a sudden it wasn't like I was carrying a gook. I was actually carrying a human being. I started feeling guilty. I just started feeling really badly.

An American soldier crouches near a dead Viet Cong.

Cong nor the Americans could do much, it seemed, except kill enemy soldiers and lose many of their own.

To break this deadlock, North Vietnam's top military leader, General Vo Nguyen Giap, conceived a major assault that he hoped would prove as devastating to the Americans as the battle of Dien Bien Phu had been for the French. It was time, he decided, for the North Vietnamese to take the offensive.

The Communists Take the Offensive

The great Communist assault came in January 1968 during the Vietnamese Lunar New Year holiday called Tet. For most Vietnamese, Tet was a festive time when families gathered to feast, celebrate with fireworks, and honor their ancestors. In the past, both North and South Vietnam had abided by a cease-fire during the Tet holiday. So, the ARVN relaxed its guard and sent many troops home to be with their families to celebrate the holiday.

Though the ARVN canceled all furloughs for troops stationed in the northern regions of South Vietnam, where a growing concentration of enemy troops was forming, half of all ARVN troops and national police in the South went on leave. General Giap expected this to happen and planned a massive attack against all major cities and towns in South Vietnam. It was the most determined and expensive military gamble taken by the Communists so far.

The first attack occurred at the U.S. marine base at Khe Sanh, an installation located not far from the Demilitarized Zone (DMZ) that separated South and North Vietnam at the seventeenth parallel. Within days an estimated fifty thousand North Vietnam regulars besieged the base and forced American commanders to send for reinforcements from elsewhere in Vietnam.

When the Communist offensive began, American officials were not totally unprepared. Westmoreland knew from intelligence reports that Giap intended a major assault, but neither he nor his advisers expected the magnitude of the Communist operation. The fighting proved so intense that many American analysts believed Giap intended Khe Sanh as the major target.

But they were wrong. Once again, Giap managed, as he often had, to draw American forces away from the populated areas to do battle on his terms. While fighting raged at Khe Sanh and other bases nearby, tens of thousands of specially trained Communist troops sneaked unnoticed into almost every major city and town in South Vietnam. They arrived on foot or rode motorbikes and bicycles, joining thousands of Vietnamese who streamed into urban areas to celebrate Tet. Most Viet Cong dressed as peasants, but bolder ones donned the uniforms of South Vietnamese soldiers and hitched rides with unsuspecting Americans into the urban areas. Once inside the cities, they gathered at designated spots such as churches and pagodas, where they opened

Dodging enemy fire, marines board a helicopter gunship at Khe Sanh.

coffins filled with guns or dug up weapons buried in cemeteries.

The Communists launched their first armed attacks just before dawn on January 30 in Da Nang, Pleiku, and six other cities. The next night the offensive expanded when seventy thousand Viet Cong and North Vietnamese soldiers attacked over one hundred major cities and hamlets. These targets included three-fourths of South Vietnam's forty-four provincial capitals.

One of the main targets was Saigon. In this capital city, forty-five hundred Viet Cong buttoned the top of their white shirts or donned red armbands to signify they belonged to the Viet Cong and fanned out across the city. Some troops were so confident of victory they spilled into the streets wearing their military uniforms.

The sound of crackling gunfire greeted the morning sunrise as the Viet Cong fired upon American military police and members of the Saigon police. Meanwhile, other commandos struck other military installations in the area. Communist forces also assailed other sites. A suicide squad attacked Saigon's Independence Palace, while other Communist troops blasted the ARVN's headquarters. Even the U.S. Embassy became a battleground when nineteen Communist commandos in civilian clothes stormed the compound and battled with marine guards, who fought continuously for five hours.

These early attacks created chaos everywhere. Terrified parents carried their children through the streets as bodies fell around them. Hospitals overflowed with the wounded, and blood supplies fell dangerously low. Recalls Tom Durant, an American civilian doctor in Saigon to help South Vietnam's medical corps:

Cho Rai is the biggest hospital in Saigon. And there was no communications between hospitals except by telephone, which was practically impossible. So you had people, ambulances going thorough, cutting through firing lines and getting shot

Broken Bodies

In *The Vietnam Reader,* edited by Stewart O'Nan, Anne Simon Auger reveals the horrors of war she experienced as an army nurse in Vietnam. The passage is extracted from Keith Walker's *A Piece of My Heart,* a book focusing on women veterans.

I was assigned to intensive care and recovery, which is like jumping into the fire. I had no preparation for it. I was six months out of nursing school and had worked in a newborn nursery until I joined the Army. It was hectic. It was fast paced. It was depressing. . . . I had been there a few months, long enough to get numb and build a few walls. This eighteen-year-old GI came into my recovery ward. He had been in an APC [armored personnel carrier] that ran over a mine, and I think he was the only survivor. He was just a young kid; I don't even think he had hair on his face yet. And he came out of the anesthesia crying for his mother. I felt so helpless. I was barely older than he was, and he's crying, "Mommy! Mommy! Mommy!" I didn't know what to do. . . . I just held him, and I think that's all

I did. It worked, but it was a real experience for me because I certainly wasn't maternal at the time and hadn't thought that would ever come up. It got me to realize how young and innocent and how naive these poor kids were. And their choices had been taken away from them.

. . . [Another patient was] . . . John. He was twenty-one. He'd gotten married before he came to Vietnam. And he was shot in his face. He absolutely lost his entire face from ear to ear. He had no nose. He was blind. It didn't matter, I guess, because he was absolutely a vegetable. He was alive and breathing; tubes and machines were keeping him alive . . . I just . . . couldn't handle it. To think of how one instant had affected his life. . . .

After John left [for Japan] I just couldn't handle it any more. We had too many bodies lying in those beds minus arms and legs, genitals, and faces, and things like that can't be put back together again.

at. It was total chaos and that was probably the major problem. . . . [W]e had four hundred wounded that day. Cho Rai Hospital became totally functionless because twenty thousand refugees moved in.[31]

As U.S. forces struggled to restore order in Saigon, another major assault was well underway in the twenty-two-hundred-year-old imperial capital of Hue in Central Vietnam, where Communists rampaged through the streets and killed priests, civil servants, teachers, American troops, and any young man of military age. As many as twenty-eight hundred residents died in the house-to-house carnage. Many victims were burned alive.

The Communist attacks provoked horror and terror throughout the city. Everywhere people ran from the fighting or huddled in fear in their homes. While they slaughtered their victims, Communists implored local residents to rise up against the Americans and the South Vietnamese government and support their new so-called liberators. Some did respond. Many college professors and students, along with crowds of Buddhists, rioted in the street to show their support.

Across South Vietnam, fierce fighting—much of it hand-to-hand combat—raged for weeks as United States and ARVN forces battled to take back Saigon, Hue, and all the other urban areas of South Vietnam under attack. Though the Communists fought hard they eventually yielded to American

firepower everywhere. House by house, street by street, U.S. forces and their allies engaged in bitter, bloody fighting, slowly reclaiming the cities of South Vietnam and ridding them of Communist aggressors. By February 25, the siege was over.

But big problems remained. Death and destruction were widespread. Hue lay in rubble, its buildings charred and collapsed. The fighting had destroyed as much as 70 percent of the fabled city. U.S. troops inflicted much of the property damage when they decided the only way to root out Communist insurgents was to demolish vast areas of the city with artillery fire.

In the aftermath of the Tet offensive, an estimated forty-five thousand North Vietnamese and Viet Cong soldiers lay dead. The U.S. claimed losses of nearly four thousand troops. In addition, hundreds of thousands of homeless South Vietnamese roamed the streets of the war-torn cities in shock, many of them mangled, stunned, and grief-stricken. At least seven thousand civilians died in the fighting.

Lessons Learned

Although the Americans had stopped the Communist offensive, all sides in the conflict learned important lessons. Giap had shown that his troops had the will and the power to move the fighting from the countryside to any place they chose. No one in South Vietnam was safe anymore. He also proved to the Americans that the Communists were willing to lose many lives to achieve their goals.

On the other hand, Communists realized they could not liberate those who did not want to be freed of the Americans. Despite their attacks, the Communists ruled only the countryside, while the United States still had the power to control the cities. Americans also demonstrated that they could not be driven out as the French had been. In addition, the Communists also realized that America's superior technology and fire power gave them the fighting edge.

Nonetheless, the Communists inflicted great damage on the United States' mission in South Vietnam. Americans at home

Soldiers use a tank as a shield against Communist rifle fire in the house-by-house, street-by-street fighting in Saigon.

viewed the bloody street fighting as a disturbing sign that things were not going well. Televised images of the Tet offensive convinced many Americans that their nation could not control events in Vietnam. Television also graphically portrayed much of the gore of killing wrought by the war. One haunting image in particular seemed to underscore this. Recalls Eddie Adams of the Associated Press, who, along with an

NBC-TV crew, photographed intense fighting in Cholon during the Tet offensive:

> As the fighting died down, we started to walk to our car, parked two blocks away. In front of us, the Vietnamese police had just captured a Vietcong lieutenant minutes after he killed a policeman. I followed them, and went to a street corner. There, General Nguyen Ngoc Loan [chief of the national police] walked over and shot him in the head. Then he turned to us and said, "They killed many of my men—and many of yours." [32]

Adams snapped a picture of the execution as General Loan fired into the man's head. The resulting photograph appeared worldwide. Though it portrayed only one of the many horrible deaths occurring in Vietnam, this image managed to convey to many people the ongoing, shocking brutality of the war.

General Nguyen Ngoc Loan, the chief of the national police, executes a Viet Cong lieutenant on February 1, 1968, during the Tet offensive. This news photograph appeared worldwide and represented to many people the brutality of the Vietnam War.

A Turning Point

Despite its military victory, the United States suffered a great psychological blow from the Tet offensive that paved the way for the long American withdrawal from Vietnam. Many Americans were now convinced that even though the United States could defeat the enemy, it could not make it cower or negotiate.

President Johnson too concluded the war had reached an impasse. He ordered a halt to the bombing and implored the leaders of North Vietnam and the Viet Cong to negotiate with the United States and South Vietnam in Paris. They accepted the offer.

At first, many U.S. troops were buoyed by the news of the talks. They believed that since the United States had won the Tet offensive the war was almost over. The upcoming talks in Paris seemed just a matter of ironing out technical details.

But negotiations proved to be a sham when they finally got underway on January 25, 1969. None of the negotiators were willing to compromise. Hostility and distrust ran rampant at the conference table. In addition, the Communists realized that rushing to an agreement with their enemy made little sense, because now another war was disturbing American society. An antiwar movement threatened to divide the nation.

Chapter 5

The War at Home

At the start of the American involvement in Vietnam, opposition was rare. But by the end of the decade, the nation reeled from the biggest antiwar movement in American history. Millions of citizens from many walks of life opposed the war. Students, professors, journalists, scientists, clergymen, business people, homemakers, and even many Vietnam War veterans rose up against their nation's activities in Vietnam. By the end of the 1960s, the antiwar movement was so widespread and disruptive that many observers believed civil war was close at hand. This antagonism to American military policy, however, did not spring from the Vietnam War alone. Its roots ran deeper—much deeper.

Roots of Dissent

The antiwar crusade was never a well-organized or clearly defined mass movement. Rather, it was a patchwork of many special interest groups with a variety of philosophies and goals. Among the first to protest the war were pacifist organizations such as the Protestant Fellowship of Reconciliation (FOR), the Quaker American Friends Service Committee (AFSC), the War Resister's League (WRL), and the Women's International League for Peace and Freedom (WILPF). Acting on moral principles, these groups had opposed all wars since the end of World War I on the grounds that killing human beings was immoral.

Fear of nuclear war motivated others to protest. In 1945 many Americans were horrified and shocked when the United States destroyed the Japanese cities of Nagasaki and Hiroshima with atomic bombs. Though these bombs ended World War II by forcing Japan's surrender, they also heralded a frightening new era of weaponry that threatened to annihilate all human life.

When the United States and the Soviet Union embarked on a nuclear arms race in the 1950s, many American groups spoke

Hiroshima lies devastated after the atomic bomb attack. Fear of nuclear war motivated some people to protest the Vietnam War.

out against what they saw as "nuclear madness." Among them were the Committee for a Sane Nuclear Policy (SANE) and the Federation of American Scientists (FAS). By the mid-1960s, SANE and FAS, along with others, began to view the Vietnam War with alarm. They feared it might trigger a larger, nuclear war between the United States and the Communist nations, China and the Soviet Union.

Another source of dissent came from the American civil rights movement. Angered by racism in American society, millions of African Americans, along with white supporters, crusaded across the country to elevate the status and civil rights of blacks and other minorities. But their struggles also convinced many activists to oppose the Vietnam War. Some saw no reason why American blacks should fight for democracy and freedom abroad when they were denied the same rights at home. In a 1967 sermon in New York, civil rights leader Dr. Martin Luther King Jr. asserted:

[The Vietnam War] was doing far more than devastating the hopes of the poor at home. It was sending their sons and their brothers and their husbands to fight and to die in extraordinarily high proportions relative to the rest of the population. We were taking the young black men who had been crippled by our society and sending them 8,000 miles away to guarantee liberties in Southeast Asia which they had not found in Southwest Georgia and East Harlem. So we have been repeatedly faced with the cruel irony of watching Negro and white boys on TV screens as they kill and die together for a nation that has been unable to seat them together in the same schools.[33]

Some dissenters even claimed Vietnamese and American blacks were natural allies because both were "colored victims" of white American racism. Although many civil rights leaders hesitated to go this far, they did believe the United States lacked the resources to fight a war and address vexing social and economic problems at the same time.

Early Vietnam War Protests

The first major, organized antiwar rally occurred in New York City in 1963 and was put together by Thomas Cornell, a member of the Catholic Worker Movement. A year later Cornell, two Roman Catholic priests, Daniel and Philip Berrigan, and others formed a group called the Catholic Peace Fellowship to protest the Vietnam War.

Soon more people rallied against the war. Among them were the Quaker's Friends Committee on National Legisla-

tion, groups opposed to Diem's regime, and SANE. They argued that the Vietnam War jeopardized relations with China and the Soviet Union and damaged attempts to negotiate limits on the nuclear arms race. Criticism also came from some government officials. Senator Mike Mansfield of Montana warned the nation against getting bogged down in an Asian war.

A variety of reasons motivated these early dissenters. Some saw American involvement in Vietnam as morally wrong. No amount of bloodshed was worth America's political goals, they argued. Others denied the United States was helping preserve democracy and freedom in Vietnam. They believed Diem's government was repressive, authoritative, and undeserving of American help. Some protesters believed Vietnam was simply too far away and served no American interest. Some war opponents complained the war was also illegal because it lacked proper congressional approval. Yet other critics claimed U.S. involvement in the war contradicted American ideals of a nation's right to self determination.

Despite their criticisms, however, few dissenters favored a one-sided American pullout. For one thing, many supported Johnson's push for civil rights legislation and were reluctant to anger him by criticizing him too harshly on Vietnam. Instead, most demanded a "negotiated settlement" and called upon the United Nations to intervene in Vietnam. This was the main theme expressed in March 1964, when five

Dr. Martin Luther King Jr. Speaks Out Against the War

Though reluctant at first to criticize America's war effort in Vietnam, Dr. Martin Luther King Jr., a winner of the 1964 Nobel Peace Prize, eventually joined the antiwar movement. In this excerpt taken from his sermon, "Beyond Vietnam," given on April 4, 1967, King tells the clergy and congregation at Riverside Church in New York City that it is time for America to end the war.

> Somehow this madness must cease. We must stop now. I speak as a child of God and brother to the suffering poor of Vietnam. I speak for those whose land is being laid waste, whose homes are being destroyed, whose culture is being subverted. I speak for the poor of America who are paying the double price of smashed hopes at home, and death and corruption in Vietnam. I speak as a citizen of the world, for the world as it stands aghast at the path we have taken. I speak as one who loves America, to the leaders of our own nation: The great initiative in this war is ours; the initiative to stop it must be ours.

This is the message of the great Buddhist leaders of Vietnam. Recently one of them wrote these words, and I quote:

> Each day the war goes on the hatred increases in the hearts of the Vietnamese and in the hearts of those of humanitarian instinct. The Americans are forcing even their friends into becoming their enemies. It is curious that the Americans, who calculate so carefully on the possibilities of military victory, do not realize that in the process they are incurring deep psychological and political defeat. The image of America will never again be the image of revolution, freedom, and democracy, but the image of violence and militarism.

If we continue, there will be no doubt in my mind and in the mind of the world that we have no honorable intentions in Vietnam. If we do not stop our war against the people of Vietnam immediately, the world will be left with no other alternative than to see this as some horrible, clumsy, and deadly game we have decided to play. The world now demands a maturity of America that we may not be able to achieve. It demands that we admit that we have been wrong from the beginning of our adventure in Vietnam, that we have been detrimental to the life of the Vietnamese people. The situation is one in which we must be ready to turn sharply from our present ways. In order to atone for our sins and errors in Vietnam, we should take the initiative in bringing a halt to this tragic war.

Dr. Martin Luther King Jr. gives his "Beyond Vietnam" sermon.

thousand people showed up for a protest march through New York City organized by nine peace groups.

By the end of 1964, opposition to the war was still not a major social movement. No consensus existed among the dissenters. In addition, no one group or point of view dominated the protesters. This attitude changed drastically, however, when Johnson ordered retaliatory bombing strikes against North Vietnam in late February 1965. College students, who had until then paid scant attention to a faraway war that seemed to have little to do with them personally, were galvanized into action.

Protest Escalates

Before the bombing strikes began, most student activism across the country had focused not on the war in Vietnam but on racism in America and hostilities between the United States and the Communist nations. In 1962, University of Michigan activists had formed the Students for a Democratic Society (SDS), an organization intended to mobilize college students across the United States to make American society more racially tolerant. Chapters of the SDS soon appeared on other college campuses, and, for the most part, members made speeches and passed out pamphlets. Few students held parades or protest demonstrations.

That changed with commencement of the bombing strikes. Members of the SDS from the University of California at Berkeley swarmed across an army railroad terminal in

Oakland and unsuccessfully tried to block the movement of military trains. The students were not alone in their protest. Though opinion polls showed that most Americans supported Johnson's action, angry dissenters went to work almost immediately. Three hundred mothers gathered in the nation's capital and complained to federal lawmakers about the escalation of the war. A week after the bombing raids began, three thousand protesters condemned the war at the United Nations Plaza in New York. On March 16, Alice Herz, an eighty-two-year-old Quaker, set herself on fire in Detroit to protest the killing.

But it was primarily college students who joined the antiwar movement as never before. By the end of the month, thousands of students and faculty members at one hundred campuses across the country participated in "teach-ins." These events were primarily instructional sessions that explained and criticized American involvement in Vietnam. They were also turning points in the antiwar movement. Among other things, they energized student protests and caused the number of campus picketers and demonstrators to swell across America. An estimated thirty thousand demonstrators took part in an antiwar protest held at Berkeley not long after the school's first teach-in. In addition, writes Charles DeBenedetti, a historian of the antiwar movement, "The 1965 teach-ins were significant . . . [because they] . . . legitimatized dissent at the outset of the war."[34]

Protesters march to the United Nations Plaza one week after the bombing of North Vietnam began.

The Vietnam War soon became the central rallying theme of protest at Berkeley and hundreds of other college campuses. By now thousands of young people openly condemned departments within their universities that provided basic war-related research and materials to both the federal government and corporations that produced weaponry used in Vietnam. Antiwar leaders also accused universities of promoting a culture of war by allowing military recruiters on campus and requiring male students to enroll in Reserve Officer Training Corps (ROTC) classes.

Antiwar demonstrations were local events until April 17, 1965, when the move-ment held its first national demonstration. The SDS persuaded twenty thousand people—mostly teens and young adults—to converge in Washington, D.C., to protest Johnson's decision to send combat troops to Vietnam. Even larger rallies took place on October 15 when an estimated one hundred thousand people in eighty cities and numerous countries participated in a massive protest called the International Day of Protest.

On November 2 another protester took his own life. After reading newspaper accounts of Vietnamese burned alive with American-made napalm, Norman Morrison, a thirty-two-year-old Quaker and father of three, stood outside the Pentagon, drenched himself with kerosene and lit a match. On November 9, twenty-two-year-old Roger Laporter also burned himself alive in the United Nations' Hammarskjöld Plaza in New York. Before he died in a nearby hospital, Laporter told those at his bedside, "I'm a Catholic Worker. I'm against war, all wars. I did this as a religious act."[35] Altogether, seven Americans perished from self-immolation during the war.

More protests were on the way. And they would expand in number and intensity when the federal government decided to send more and more young men to kill and die in Vietnam.

Changing the Rules

As the war expanded, the federal government's need for manpower grew. The job of adding more young men to the U.S. military system fell to the nation's Selective Service Commission (SSC). Before the Johnson years, the country's thirty-seven hundred local draft boards conscripted between six thousand and seven thousand men each month. But by early 1965 that figure rose. By April it had more than doubled. At the end of the year, forty thousand young men were being inducted into the armed forces each month.

To reach its monthly quotas, the SSC revoked many student exemptions and deferments. No longer, for example, did married students receive an exemption from military service. The SSC also tried to do away with another provision that allowed students four years to complete their education before being eligible for the draft. This provision was not eliminated but it was weakened in February 1966 when SSC director General Lewis B. Hershey announced that local draft boards could draft college students who ranked in the lower academic levels of their schools.

These policy changes ignited student protests across the nation. At the University of Chicago, SDS students urged college officials to refuse to cooperate with the SSC. They argued that the government's policy was immoral, it pitted students against one another, and it turned the university into an agency of death for the government. When school officials rebuffed their demands, four hundred angry students stormed the administration building and vowed not to leave until they got what they wanted. But the administration held firm and five days later the students left empty-handed.

Their actions, however, were not in vain. Inspired by what had happened at the University of Chicago, students elsewhere in the country staged similar sit-ins. During that same spring, Cornell University student Bruce Dancis burned his draft card and sent the ashes to his draft board. Fellow students rallied in his support and formed the nation's first of many "We Won't Go" groups that sprang up around the country and urged draft resistance. Organizers hoped massive resistance would obstruct the justice system and cause the nation to debate the war more intensely.

Many young men who received draft notices refused to report for duty and were arrested. Others ran away. Eventually, an estimated fifty thousand young men left the United States to avoid military duty and sought asylum in Canada and Sweden. They were often joined by thousands of others who had deserted the military. Most of these acts violated the law.

On March 26, 1966, a second International Day of Protest took place. This time thirty thousand Americans demonstrated in New York City, Chicago, Boston, San Francisco, and elsewhere. By now celebrities including singer Eartha Kitt, boxer Muhammad Ali, and writers Norman Mailer, Robert Lowell, Allen Ginsberg, and Arthur Miller had joined the protesters. Noted pediatrician Dr. Benjamin Spock and the Reverend William Sloan Coffin, chaplain of Yale University, along with 320 educators and intellectuals,

Students burn their draft cards during a sit-in.

signed a document that implored students to resist the draft.

Opposition also appeared in the U.S. Congress and other public institutions. In May 1966, Senator J. William Fulbright of Arkansas, who headed the Foreign Relations Committee, accused the United States of "succumbing to the arrogance of power."[36] The next month, in response to news that the United States was bombing Hanoi for the first time, the names of 6,400 people appeared in a three-page antiwar ad in the *New York Times*. Among them were the names of 3,938 college faculty members.

Later that summer many antiwar leaders decided to try a new protest tactic. Soon protesters in many cities approached anyone wearing a U.S. military uniform and urged him to refuse to participate in the war. Though most military personnel scorned such pleas, a few agreed. On July 13, 1966, three soldiers from Fort Hood, Texas, announced at a New York press conference that they would disobey their orders to report to Vietnam. A week later, federal agents arrested them. Later, the military court-martialed the three young men and sent them to prison for two years.

Wearing a tie decorated with peace symbols and doves, Dr. Benjamin Spock marches in a peace rally in New York City in 1971.

Dissension Within the Antiwar Movement

By the summer of 1966 many protest leaders wondered whether any of their tactics mattered. The U.S. government reported in September that three hundred thousand troops were now stationed in Vietnam. Death tolls were rising too. America's armed forces suffered a record 970 casualties and 145 dead in one week.

Serious internal problems also confronted the antiwar movement. Various leaders quarreled over goals and tactics. In addition, two major ideologies within the movement pitted activists against each other. One side consisted of those who for religious or philosophical reasons believed all protests should be nonviolent. Some who favored this tactic did so for practical reasons. They had observed civil rights workers use nonviolence with great success and now wished to employ it in the peace movement.

In opposition were those who scorned nonviolence as ineffectual and time consuming. They believed violence was necessary to halt the killing in Vietnam. Radicals in this faction despised American society and believed the U.S. government was corrupt and immoral. In their eyes only a revolution could end the war and create a radical change in American society. Though proponents of violence were a minority in the antiwar community, they were influential. As the war dragged on, growing numbers of dissenters adopted the methods of the radicals.

Overcoming Differences

In response to these problems, various leaders of the antiwar movement ultimately agreed to put aside their differences and create a massive coalition. On November 26, 1966, they formed the Spring Mobilization Committee to End the War in Vietnam (or Spring MOBE). This new organization invited almost anyone opposed to the war: SDS members, students, civil rights workers, religious activists, Women Strike for Peace, members of the Socialist Workers Party, Communists, and many others. For the next four months, antiwar leaders labored hard to coordinate their efforts and solicit support from the American people.

Their hard work paid off with the largest antiwar demonstration to date. On April 15, 1967, an estimated four hundred thousand people marched in New York City, while another seventy-five thousand demonstrated in San Francisco. Among those were six Vietnam veterans who had become disgusted with the war and chose

Approximately four hundred thousand protesters marched in New York City on April 15, 1967.

to side with the protesters. These veterans later formed Vietnam Veterans Against the War (VVAW), a group that became increasingly visible in the protests that followed.

Though most men and women who had served in the armed forces did not support the protests in any way, a minority of angry veterans did. In symbolic acts of protest, some openly burned their military discharge cards and heaved their battlefield medals to the ground during rallies to show their contempt for what their nation was doing.

The tension between active antiwar veterans and those still in uniform climaxed on October 21, 1967, when one hundred thousand protesters converged on the Pentagon. For the first time ever, the American public saw televised images of veterans passing out antiwar literature to uniformed soldiers and urging them to disobey orders to go to war. Even the most ardent critics of antiwar demonstrators were often hesitant to condemn this new brand of protester who had experienced the reality of war and came away horrified by it.

America in Revolt

Over time, the antiwar movement continued to grow. Even some mainstream religious organizations turned against the war. The National Council of Churches, for instance, passed a resolution calling on young men to resist the draft. Some clergymen performed individual acts of protest. Father Philip Berrigan and three others poured human blood on the Selective Service records in Baltimore's Customs House and received six-year prison sentences.

By 1968, nearly half of the country's three thousand colleges and universities reported student demonstrations of varying degrees. Such disturbances had scarcely existed three years previously. By now many of the protests were violent. Acts of civil disruption, strikes, vandalism, and rioting multiplied across the country. In March, for example, a peaceful antiwar march against the Pentagon in Washington, D.C., attended by thirty thousand turned violent when protesters confronted National Guard soldiers.

In April 1968, violence also shook Columbia University in New York when obscenity-yelling students clashed with police and occupied four administration buildings for six days. Their occupation ended when police stormed the building, beat the students, and sprayed them with tear gas. Over seven hundred were arrested and one hundred injured. Students smoldered with anger and rioted again weeks later. Once again demonstrators stormed school buildings and fought with police.

Americans from all walks of life were shocked by the violence and chaos that swept their nation. Massive civil rights demonstrations accompanied the growing antiwar protests, and many of these were violent. Riots, arson, looting, and gun battles between black militants and police became increasingly common in America. Not since the Civil War had the United States witnessed such widespread social unrest and political division. Parades, marches, demonstrations, and riots erupted across the country. Students burned their draft cards. They attacked college ROTC buildings, banks, research centers, and other facilities thought to be associated with the war effort. They demonstrated in front of local draft board offices. Many attempted to stop troop trains and block entrances to munitions factories. College students gathered outside the White House and chanted, "Hey, hey, LBJ, how many kids did you kill today?"

Though these actions dramatized the anguish of those wanting peace, they also provoked an angry response from other Americans who formed their own smaller, yet potent, counterrevolt.

Counterrevolt

Though also disturbed by the war, more-conservative Americans also believed their country had a duty to honor its commitment to protect the South Vietnamese. They also thought the antiwar protesters insulted and discouraged American troops, embarrassed the president, and aided the Communists. As army nurse Lynda Van Devanter explained to her mother in a letter from Vietnam:

It hurts so much sometimes to see the paper full of demonstrators, especially people burning the flag. Fight fire with fire, we ask here. Display the flag, Mom and Dad, please, every day. And tell your friends to do the same. It means so much to us to know we're supported, to know not everyone feels we're making a mistake being here.[37]

To counteract the antiwar movement, war supporters staged their own events. On May 13, 1967, seventy thousand marched through New York City to support the war. A "Support America's Vietnam Effort" day

An American flag is burned during an antiwar rally in Washington, D.C.

held on October 30, drew twenty-five thousand defenders of Johnson's policy. Thousands of students at universities around the country signed petitions in support of America's war effort.

Some defenders of the government used more violent means to express their outrage with the antiwar movement. In various parts of the country groups of American Nazis and the Hell's Angels, for example, beat antiwar protesters. Some extremists even killed dissenters. It was clear the nation was deeply divided, and as the 1968 presidential election approached, no end to the conflict was in sight.

Johnson Shocks the Nation

Even before 1968, key Democrats realized the Vietnam War was hurting not only the nation but also their party. Though opinion polls showed a majority of Americans still approved of Johnson's handling of the war, that support was slipping. Opinion polls showed that concern over Vietnam and the rising inflation caused by the war produced a drop of thirty-six percentage points in the president's approval rating between 1964 and 1968.

Signs were strong that Johnson might not be reelected in 1968. To keep the presidency in their control, many Democrats now supported a new candidate—Eugene McCarthy, a liberal, antiwar senator from Minnesota. Thousands of antiwar students poured into New Hampshire and campaigned for McCarthy in the party's first primary election of the campaign. On March

12, McCarthy lost to Johnson, but only by 230 votes out of 60,000 cast statewide. That a challenger had done so well against an incumbent president offered glaring proof that the president was in political trouble.

McCarthy's strong showing also encouraged another antiwar Democrat—Robert Kennedy, the popular former U.S. attorney general and brother of the slain president—to seek his party's nomination. Many political observers considered Kennedy, a man who enjoyed vast popularity among both whites and blacks, an even more serious threat to Johnson than McCarthy. And Johnson soon faced another problem. From the conservative wing of his party came another presidential contender, Governor George Wallace of Alabama. Unlike the other two challengers, Wallace demanded a stronger use of force in Vietnam.

Though dismayed by the challengers and the eroding public support for his policies, Johnson vowed to fight to win his party's nomination. During his entire political career, he had always campaigned hard and had never shrunk before a challenge. But his confidence wavered on March 26 when a group of trusted advisers and statesmen nicknamed the "Wise Men" visited him in the Oval Office. Previously many of these same men had encouraged Johnson to take military action in Vietnam. Now most of them urged him to "disengage" the nation from Vietnam. Two days later, Secretary of Defense Clark Clifford drove this point home when he saw a draft of a prowar speech Johnson intended to make.

A Follower for the Cause

In an interview with the author, former peace activist Connie Brawley recalls her days in the antiwar movement.

It was the deaths of people close to me that got me involved in the antiwar movement. First, a high school friend was killed in Vietnam. Then another friend lost control of himself during a battle in Vietnam and started shooting everywhere without regard to the location of his own men. He then had to be medically discharged. One more friend committed suicide when he came home. I didn't want any more to die, so I became a follower for the cause.

What also motivated me was hearing a conscientious objector speak on my college campus. He faced prosecution from the government for not going to Vietnam. Next to him stood his pregnant wife; I was really touched that they would have to leave the country because of the war.

At the time, I was 20 and going to junior college in St. Louis. I joined a protest group that started an anti-war newspaper called "Up Against the Wall" that we distributed in the St. Louis area. We also staged sit-ins and picketed the local draft board. I was always peaceful in my protests. But others weren't. I remember one night during a rally somebody set a fire in the Washington University R.O.T.C. building.

Our antiwar group was also involved in the planning for the first big moratorium in Washington D.C. in 1969. There was a lot of work to do. Finally, we traveled to Washington in eight buses and stayed for three days in apartments of complete strangers who opened their homes to us.

We were among a quarter of a million people who came from all over America to attend rallies and hear speeches taking place at the Washington Monument. Except for one place, Dupont Circle, where a radical group—the SDS—got tear-gassed, the moratorium was mostly peaceful. In fact, it was the most organized and peaceful experience for something so large that I'd ever attended.

Mostly college kids were there, but I did see older people who I thought must have had their own children over in Vietnam.

One day, a Washington D.C. cop came up to me and pulled his collar over and showed me a peace sign. It was his way of showing us he was on our side.

After that moratorium, I stayed active in the anti-war movement until 1973. I don't think my parents ever approved of what I did in those days. They were from the World War II generation and they didn't understand mine. But Jessica, my own grown daughter, I think, was proud of me when she heard of my experiences. I feel like I was doing the right thing and I think we made a difference in bringing about an end to the war. I also felt important to be part of a common cause and to make history.

Clifford complained to Secretary of State Dean Rusk:

The president cannot give that speech! It would be a disaster! What seems not to be understood is that major elements of the national constituency—the business community, the press, the churches, the professional groups, college presidents, students, and most of

the intellectual community—turned against this war. What the President
needs is not a war speech, but a peace
speech.[38]

Clifford's words convinced Rusk to di-
rect his staff to write a more conciliatory
speech to be delivered on March 31. In a
televised address, Johnson announced a
bombing halt in North Vietnam, except in
areas where Communist troops posed a
threat to Americans and South Vietnamese.
He also implored the leaders of North Vietnam to engage in peace negotiations. And
then he concluded his statement with an
announcement that stunned the nation:

> There is divisiveness among us all
> tonight. And holding the trust that is
> mine, as President of all the people, I
> cannot disregard the peril to the
> progress of the American people and
> the hope and prospect of peace for all
> people.
>
> . . . With America's sons in the fields far
> away, with America's future under chal-
> lenge right here at home . . . I do not
> believe that I should devote an hour or
> a day of my time to any personal parti-
> san causes. . . . Accordingly, I shall not
> seek, and will not accept, the nomina-
> tion of my party for another term as
> your President.[39]

With Johnson out of the presidential
race, the stage was set for a raucous debate

at the Democratic National Convention in
Chicago that summer. Here the Democrats
would wrangle not only over who their candidate would be, but also over what course
of action the nation should take in Vietnam.

Antiwar activists across the nation also
had their eyes on Chicago. They, too,
planned to be there and to make their
views on Vietnam known to the world.

Days of Rage in Chicago

Chicagoans were on edge when an assort-
ment of protest groups showed up in August. For weeks, local newspapers had
circulated alarming stories that arriving dissenters meant to cause chaos in Chicago's
streets. Some of these reports were mere rumors. But others were based on statements
made by radical dissenters. Some radicals,
for example, threatened to run wild in the
streets and to spike Chicago's water supply
with LSD, a potent hallucinogenic drug.

In addition to the radicals, MOBE,
SDS, the Women Strike for Peace, the National Lawyer's Guild, and many other
groups and individuals came to Chicago.
Altogether, nearly ten thousand demonstrators arrived to protest the war.

Tension mounted when dissenters
learned Chicago authorities would not
grant them permits to have peaceful
marches or rallies. Many vowed to demonstrate anyway. Richard Daley, the gruff, no-
nonsense mayor of Chicago, was ready for
them. At his disposal were twelve thousand
police, seventy-five hundred U.S. Army
troops and six thousand National Guards-

men. Violence broke out on the evening of August 24 when police clubbed and tear-gassed protesters, reporters, and passersby after thousands of demonstrators refused to leave Lincoln Park at the 11 P.M. curfew.

Conditions inside the convention hall were scarcely more civil. Squabbling and fistfights broke out among the Democrats over questions of minority representation among the delegations from Georgia and Alabama. Zealous security forces often beat delegates and reporters on the convention floor to keep order.

Amid this turmoil, Democratic Party leaders struggled to conduct debates on issues vital to the party. Not until 2 A.M. did they bring up the topic on everybody's mind. As authors Carl Dougan and Samuel Lipsman put it, "The first full-scale debate on the war in Vietnam held by any regularly constituted institution of American politics is to take place while two-thirds of the nation is fast asleep."[40] Three days later violence broke out again. On the convention floor, speakers argued vehemently over the war, as delegates shouted, booed, and jeered. Once again, security guards beat people in the convention hall.

Trouble brewed in the streets too. At 7:15 P.M. many antiwar protesters tried to join a peaceful march led by a black civil rights group that possessed a city permit. When police tried to keep the protesters from advancing along with the legitimate marchers, a riot broke out. Soon, police plunged into the crowd, wielding billy clubs. Angry protesters fought back, threw rocks, and yelled obscenities. As television cameras whirred, demonstrators chanted, "The whole world is watching! The whole world is watching."[41] Two hours later, CBS News interrupted proceedings at the convention to show the audience a film sequence of the violence that had occurred on Chicago's streets. Delegates, along with millions of television viewers, were aghast.

When the convention ended the next day, Hubert Humphrey, Johnson's vice president, was the party's nominee for the upcoming general election in November. He tried hard to unite his party, but his decision to continue Johnson's policy in Vietnam infuriated McCarthy delegates. The split in the Democratic Party over Vietnam was so deep that it divided Democrats for years. As then Senator George McGovern of South Dakota later observed: "The Viet Nam tragedy is at the root of the confusion and division of the Democratic Party. It tore up our souls."[42]

With the Democratic Party in disarray and sullied by events in Chicago, Humphrey could do little to capture the confidence of a majority of voters. In November, Americans elected as their next president Republican Richard Nixon—a man who claimed he had a "secret plan" for ending the Vietnam War.

Chapter 6

Nixon Takes Charge

When Richard Nixon assumed the presidency on January 20, 1969, the Vietnam War continued to disrupt and divide the American people. As Nixon observed in his inaugural speech, "We are caught in war, wanting peace. We're torn by divisions, wanting unity. We see around us empty lives, wanting fulfillment."[43]

A native Californian, Nixon was an intelligent, conniving, ambitious man who began his career in politics in the late 1940s as a fierce anti-Communist. A trained lawyer and a conservative Republican, Nixon served as a U.S. congressman before becoming Eisenhower's vice president in the 1950s. After a narrow loss to Kennedy in the 1960 presidential race and a second defeat in a California gubernatorial race, he vowed to leave politics forever. That did not happen. Instead, he became president.

Though opinion polls showed a growing number of Americans in late 1968 considered U.S. involvement in Vietnam a big

mistake and wanted it to end, Nixon had no intention of pulling out U.S. troops without major concessions from the enemy. He knew his country might not win the war, but he had no intention of losing. What he pledged instead was "peace with honor."

For help, Nixon turned to Henry Kissinger, his national security adviser. Kissinger was a German Jew who emigrated to the United States in 1938 to avoid Nazi persecution in Germany. Considered brilliant, hardworking, and ruthless by both friends and foes, Kissinger eventually obtained a Ph.D. at Harvard University, where he taught history before going to work for the federal government. An expert on the history of international diplomacy, he believed negotiations between hostile nations succeeded only when a settlement assured the security of all parties involved. But he thought such agreements seldom took place when negotiators relied on public opinion to make decisions. In Kissinger's view the public was often unwilling to compromise with foreign countries. Therefore, he said, it was important to negotiate secretly.

Kissinger also held a unique view on the Vietnam War. He argued that the United States had already demonstrated its ability to prevent North Vietnam from seizing the South. And this exhibition of power had maintained American prestige in the international community. But the United States had not created a government in South Vietnam strong enough to stand alone against the Communists. Kissinger believed this situation was not a big problem, because the United States had no lasting obligation to be the guardian of Vietnam. What was important was how the United States comported itself when it left Vietnam. Nixon understood the importance of what Kissinger said. He had no plans to simply abandon a U.S. ally. Instead, the president resolved to enable South Vietnam to survive on its own before the Americans left.

As Kissinger and Nixon hammered out their foreign policy, widespread fighting persisted in Vietnam. On February 22, 1969, the Communists launched another Tet offensive. Once again, they struck many of South Vietnam's forty-four provincial capitals. They also attacked several American military bases and killed 1,140 Americans.

President Richard Nixon (left) relied on his national security adviser, Henry Kissinger, to achieve "peace with honor" in Vietnam.

The attack angered Nixon, who believed it violated an understanding the Communists reached with Johnson when he halted all bombing on November 1, 1968. America's top leader wanted retaliation, and the place he had in mind to carry it out was in Vietnam's neighbor, Cambodia.

Bombing Campaign in Cambodia

At this time, Cambodia was a mostly rural country ruled by a flamboyant prince named Norodom Sihanouk. Fearful that the Vietnam War would spill over Vietnam's borders into his own country, Sihanouk had professed Cambodia's neutrality to prevent antagonizing any of the warring groups. As he once put it: "We are a country caught between the hammer and the anvil, a country that would very much like to remain the last haven of peace in Southeast Asia."[44]

Despite his avowed neutrality, Sihanouk made concessions to both the Communists and the Americans. To keep the North Vietnamese happy, he allowed Communist forces to amass weapons depots and other military camps along his nation's border with Vietnam. The Viet Cong used these sites to launch raids against Americans and their allies in Vietnam. But the prince also agreed to allow U.S. troops to enter his country if they were in "hot pursuit" of Viet Cong troops seeking sanctuary in Cambodia. The United States took advantage of this permission for years.

Now desiring stronger measures against the Communists, Nixon decided upon an intensive bombing of Communist bases in Cambodia. The purpose of the raids was to hinder the ability of the Communists to slip across the border into South Vietnam and attack ARVN and American troops. Nixon also hoped the bombing campaign would wipe out the Central Office of South Vietnam (COSVN), a Communist headquarters believed to exist near the Vietnamese border.

On March 18, 1969, American B-52 bombers pounded Communist sanctuaries in Cambodia. Nixon and his advisers knew the attacks would anger the enemy, but they also believed the Communists were unlikely to complain publicly and draw attention to the fact that they had bases in Cambodia. Nor was Sihanouk likely to speak out and reveal that he permitted the Communists to operate freely within his country and therefore endanger South Vietnam.

Despite these expectations, the Nixon administration kept the bombing raids secret in hopes of preventing a wild outburst from the antiwar movement. Even the secretary of the Air Force, the Air Force chief of staff, and most of Congress knew nothing about the mission, dubbed "Operation Menu."

The secrecy effort failed. Two months later, a British journalist who was in Cambodia broke the story in the *New York Times*. The revelation, however, failed to generate the public outrage many U.S. officials expected. But the bombing also disappointed America's war planners. The destruction wreaked by American firepower did little to curtail Communist activity along the Vietnamese border. Nor did it do much to hinder North Vietnam's overall determination to wage war against South Vietnam.

On the other hand, the Communists were in no position to oust the Americans. Nixon had demonstrated a willingness to use devastating air power. In effect, the war

At an air base in Guam, B-52s are prepared for a bombing mission over Cambodia.

had reached another stalemate. Yet another impasse was underway in Paris, where the peace talks between the Americans, South Vietnam, North Vietnam, and the Viet Cong—begun during the end of the Johnson Administration—were going nowhere. North Vietnam insisted on the withdrawal of U.S. troops from Vietnam and the removal of the government in Saigon. The Communists wanted a new government for Vietnam determined by free elections that would include Communist representatives. The Americans and the South Vietnamese wanted no part of such an arrangement.

A New Policy

Melvin Laird, Nixon's new secretary of state, urged Nixon to do something to break the deadlock. An astute political observer, Laird argued that Congress was unlikely to fund other important national defense needs if lawmakers perceived the United States was accomplishing little or nothing in Vietnam. Therefore, he urged the president to implement a new policy that was first conceived in the Johnson administration.

Known as "Vietnamization," this policy consisted of three steps. First, the United States would turn over most combat missions to the ARVN, while still providing air and logistical support. Next, the Americans would strengthen the fighting capability of the ARVN. Finally, U.S. military personnel would remain in Vietnam but restrict themselves to serving as advisers, not soldiers. Lacking a secret plan to end the war that he had promised in his campaign, Nixon embraced Vietnamization. Now he had a way to slowly extract Americans from the fighting but not appear to abandon an ally. He left implementation of Vietnamization to General Creighton W. Abrams, the new commander who replaced Westmoreland in 1968.

Under the first phase of Vietnamization, vast amounts of new weapons and millions of dollars for new military training programs flowed into Vietnam in 1969. By the end of the year, the size of the ARVN had doubled to more than 1 million. None of these actions meant the Americans were leaving Vietnam anytime soon. Though the South Vietnamese slowly took over more of the ground war, the United States continued bombing raids. But the Communists showed no signs of yielding to American military force.

Frustrated, Nixon instructed Kissinger to ask the Soviet Union to put pressure on the North Vietnamese to compromise with the Americans. But the Soviets were either unwilling or unable to do so. Next, the president appeared on television on May 14 and suggested the Americans and North Vietnamese mutually withdraw their troops from South Vietnamese soil. Both sides would exchange prisoners of war. In addition, free elections would take place in South Vietnam. The president also implied that the Americans intended to reduce their role in Vietnam: "The time is approaching when the South Vietnamese forces will be able to take over some of the fighting fronts now being manned by Americans,"[45] he said.

North Vietnamese officials in Hanoi promptly rebuffed Nixon's offer. For one thing, they considered their troops as the military wing of the legitimate government in all of Vietnam and resented being equated with the American intruders. Besides, they saw no reason to agree to withdraw troops because Americans planned to withdraw troops under Vietnamization anyway.

On June 8, Nixon met South Vietnam's president, Nguyen Van Thieu, at the Pacific island of Midway, where antiwar demonstrators were unlikely to mar the meeting. Nixon had decided it was time to implement another phase of Vietnamization. "I have decided to order the immediate redeployment from Vietnam of the divisional equivalent of approximately 25,000 men,"[46] the president announced. Nixon added that another 40,000 would depart in three months.

Though American involvement was far from over, summer brought a lull in the fighting in South Vietnam, although U.S. officials were unsure why. They did understand, by now, however, that the secret bombings of the supply lines in Cambodia were not going to end the war.

Another lull occurred that summer: The number of antiwar protests in the

United States dwindled. But Nixon's staff believed this lull was only temporary. They knew antiwar activities would increase when schools reopened in September. Congress would also be back in session, and many representatives were expected to present bills that demanded a pullout of U.S. military forces in Vietnam. The Nixon administration had yet another worry. U.S. military intelligence revealed that the Communists were likely to launch a major attack on South Vietnam in February 1970.

Amid these pressures, Nixon concluded he had to do something dramatic. He decided to "go for broke" and end the war "either by negotiated agreement or by

ARVN soldiers pose with their American-supplied tank. The first phase of Vietnamization began in 1969.

an increased use of force."[47] So he ordered Kissinger, who was now negotiating secretly with North Vietnamese delegates in France, to send an ultimatum to the Communists. If they did not comply by November 1 with the peace proposals made during his May 14 speech, he would be "compelled—with great reluctance—to take measures of the greatest consequences."[48]

Meanwhile, Nixon's staff prepared plans for a backup plan called "Duck Hook" in case the Communists refused. They envisioned another round of massive bombing attacks on North Vietnam and a possible land invasion. Some staff members even developed a plan to use nuclear weaponry to destroy the Ho Chi Minh Trail, if necessary.

To the relief of many war planners, Nixon chose not to order massive retaliation when Ho rejected his ultimatum on August 30. What most likely swayed the president were dire predictions from cautious staffers that a massive attack in Vietnam would provoke enormous and wild

American soldiers move out on patrol as their helicopter transports depart. President Nixon decided to end the war by an increased use of force.

antiwar protests at home. Soon afterward, startling news came from Hanoi on September 5: Ho Chi Minh was dead, at the age of seventy-nine. In his last testament, he predicted that though a hard struggle still remained, his country would eventually beat the Americans:

No matter what difficulties and hardships lie ahead, our people are sure of total victory. The US imperialists will certainly have to quit. Our Fatherland will certainly be reunified. Our fellow-countrymen in the South and in the North will certainly be re-united under the same roof. We, a small nation, will have earned the single honour of defeating, through heroic struggle, two big imperialisms—the French and the American—and of making a worthy contribution to the world national-liberation movement.[49]

As the North Vietnamese mourned the loss of their leader, the Nixon administration faced disturbing questions: Who would now lead the Communists? Would North Vietnam's war policies change? Were chances for peace improved or lessened by Ho's death? Some veteran Vietnam observers predicted that without Ho's powerful presence, North Vietnam's other leaders would fight among themselves and slow the Communist drive into South Vietnam.

Nixon and his advisers pondered these questions as millions of students poured back onto America's college campuses.

Many had spent the summer preparing for the biggest antiwar protest yet. Now they were ready to act.

More Protests

By now, many antiwar leaders believed the antiwar movement should no longer be confined primarily to college campuses. Instead, they proposed hosting a series of "moratoriums" to be held one day each month in cities and towns across the nation. The purpose of the moratoriums was to bring normal day-to-day activities to a halt and replace them with massive protests against the war.

The first moratorium took place at multiple sites on October 15. At least one million Americans nationwide demonstrated with candlelight processions and prayer vigils in San Francisco, Boston, Miami, Detroit, New York, and other U.S. cities. Protesters also assembled in London, Paris, Tokyo, Sydney, and Dublin. Even some U.S. soldiers stationed in Vietnam expressed opposition to the war by wearing black armbands.

The moratorium angered and worried Nixon. Keeping a low profile himself, he allowed his vice president, Spiro Agnew, to verbally attack the antiwar movement in order to discredit it. Resorting to exaggeration and name-calling, Agnew lambasted dissenters and news-gathering organizations that criticized the administration's war aims. He inflamed his critics when he called antiwar leaders "an effete corps of impudent snobs."[50]

Keenly aware that war protests had helped to drive Johnson from office, Nixon decided to take a more active role to protect his own political career. On November 3, before the next moratorium, he spoke to the nation and announced his "plan to end the war" which, for the most part, rehashed the goals of Vietnamization. Nixon also claimed he was willing to compromise with the Communists if they recognized South Vietnam as a legitimate independent nation. However, he also threatened to use force if they escalated the war.

Nixon's popularity soared after his speech. On November 11, Veteran's Day, many American citizens demonstrated in support of the president. But his words made no impact on the war protesters. Instead, antiwar fever grew as a result of the recent revelation that during the Tet offensive the previous year, U.S. troops had, without provocation, slaughtered more than three hundred South Vietnamese—mostly women and children—at My Lai, a village in the Quangngai province of South Vietnam.

Meanwhile, the Vietnam War showed no signs of slowing down. Predictions of a leadership crisis in North Vietnam caused by Ho Chi Minh's death proved false. Instead, as author Stanley Karnow points out, "His mantle now fell on old warriors like Le Duan, Pham Van Dong, and Vo Nguyen Giap, nationalists who had been fighting against Westerners for most of their adult lives. Like Ho, they regarded the defeat of the United States and its South Vietnamese

allies to be a sacred duty."[51] Under new leadership, Communist strength in Vietnam rebounded. By 1970 two-thirds of the 125,000 Communist troops were now North Vietnamese who had been sent to replace Viet Cong killed in the Tet offensive.

During this same period, growing numbers of American ground troops left Vietnam. Troop withdrawal, however, did not mean the United States was close to quitting Vietnam. Nixon's war planners, in fact, were preparing to expand the war into Cambodia.

The Cambodia Incursion

In the spring of 1970, a pro-U.S. faction headed by Cambodia's prime minister, Lon Nol, ousted Sihanouk when the Cambodian prince was in the Soviet Union. Fearful of the growing number of Communist troops in his country, Nol called upon his fellow Cambodians to drive them from the country. Passions inflamed, Cambodians attacked not only North Vietnamese troops but ethnic Vietnamese civilians who happened to live in Cambodia as well. Mobs rampaged across the country and slaughtered Vietnamese men, women, and children. In response, North Vietnamese troops, with help from a specially trained group of Cambodian Communist forces called the Khmer Rouge, attacked Cambodia's government troops and moved dangerously close to the country's urban areas.

With Cambodia now in chaos, Lon Nol made an international plea for help in removing the Communists. Though the

A U.S. Soldier Uncovers a Massacre

In 1968, Ronald Ridenhour, a former combat veteran in Vietnam, wrote a letter to leading members of Congress that launched the investigation of the My Lai massacre. This excerpt comes from Seymour Hersh's *My Lai 4: A Report on the Massacre and Its Aftermath.*

It was late in April, 1968, that I first heard of "Pinkville" and what allegedly happened there. I received that first report with some skepticism, but in the following months I was to hear similar stories from such a wide variety of people that it became impossible for me to disbelieve that something rather dark and bloody did occur sometime in March, 1968, in a village called "Pinkville" in the Republic of Vietnam. . . .

In late April, 1968, I was awaiting orders for a transfer . . . when I happened to run into [Charles] "Butch" Gruver [a soldier Ridenhour knew]. . . .

When "Butch" told me [that his company had been ordered to destroy all inhabitants in the village on a search-and-destroy mission] . . . I didn't quite believe that what he was telling me was true, but he assured me that it was and went on to describe what happened . . . I asked "Butch" several times if all the people were killed. He said that he thought they were, men, women, and children . . . Gruver estimated that the population of the village had been 300 to 400 people and that very few, if any, escaped.

A young Vietnamese boy mourns his slain sister, a victim of the My Lai massacre.

Nixon administration had no intention of committing itself to the defense of Cambodia, it did want to make a symbolic effort to render aid. Plus, the president and his advisers also believed the disorder in Cambodia offered an excuse for the United States to demolish the Communist sanctuaries in Cambodia that bombing had thus far failed to destroy.

At 9 P.M on April 30, 1970, Nixon addressed the nation with a surprising announcement: Americans, along with ARVN troops, were on their way into the eastern edge of Cambodia to destroy Communist sanctuaries and prevent the enemy from launching massive attacks against Vietnam. Nixon was unapologetic. "If when the chips are down, the world's most powerful nation, the United States of America, acts like a pitiful, helpless giant, the forces of totalitarianism and anarchy will threaten free nations and free institutions throughout the world."[52]

The nation was startled. Most Americans had grown accustomed to periodic announcements of American troop withdrawals and official statements that suggested the war was winding down. Now, quite suddenly, just the opposite was happening. America was at war in another Asian country.

Reaction to the Cambodian Incursion

At first, many Americans considered the U.S. incursion into Cambodia a military success. Two weeks after the American invasion, thirty thousand Americans, along with forty-eight thousand ARVN troops, had captured several Communist bases and in most cases met only mild resistance. Many Viet Cong troops slipped off into the jungles rather than fight. American troops rejoiced over the bounty of enemy war supplies they had seized: 15 million rounds of ammunition, 143,000 rockets, 22,892 separate weapons, 199,552 antiaircraft rounds, 62,000 grenades and 5,487 mines.

The South Vietnamese army also had another success. By this time, relations between Cambodia and Vietnam had deteriorated as a result of Cambodia's persecution of ethnic Vietnamese. The slaughter ceased, however, when South Vietnamese troops arrived in Cambodia. The acting head of state, Lon Nol, allowed Vietnamese soldiers to evacuate tens of thousands of Vietnamese who wished to leave the country and avoid further molestation.

But nothing that U.S. or ARVN troops did halted Communist activity for very long. The Soviet Union and China quickly reequipped North Vietnam, and supply routes to the Viet Cong soon reopened. Worse yet for the Nixon administration, the Cambodian incursion breathed new life into the American antiwar movement just when it had begun to falter. Wild protests disrupted college campuses across the country. Suspicion grew even among Nixon's supporters that the president now either meant to expand the war or win it. Some in Congress openly questioned whether Nixon had the constitutional authority to extend the war into Cambodia. Others worried that the United States now was responsible for the safety of both South Vietnam and Cambodia.

Outbursts against American policy in Vietnam were no longer confined to the young. Bankers, business people, home-makers, and other adults also demon-strated in the streets of the United States. Nor were demonstrations limited to the na-tion's big urban centers. Dissent was also growing in the more conservative and rural areas of America. Nowhere was this more tragically demonstrated than at Ohio's Kent State University.

Four Dead in Ohio

What began as a peaceful antiwar demon-stration by three hundred students on Fri-day, May 1, turned violent when students rampaged in the town of Kent. On Saturday,

the campus ROTC building went up in flames. The situation worsened when a crowd of onlookers refused to make way for firefighters when they arrived. Infuriated by these events, Ohio governor James Rhodes dispatched nine hundred National Guard troops to restore order at the university.

On Monday, one thousand Kent State students defied a ban on student demon-strations and staged another antiwar rally on campus. Armed with pistols and machine guns, guardsmen tried to break up the rally. Students reacted with jeers and obscenities. Some battered troops with rocks and pieces of concrete as others cheered. Suddenly, guardsmen fired into the crowd for thirteen seconds, killing four students and wounding

At Kent State, students flee as National Guard troops open fire at an antiwar rally on May 1, 1970.

nine. Some of the victims were merely on their way to class and were not taking part in the demonstration.

The Kent State killings traumatized Americans. Public protests erupted immediately. On May 8, one hundred thousand people marched on Washington, D.C. Violent clashes between students and police took place on more than two dozen campuses. Nixon inflamed the situation when his press secretary read a statement on behalf of the president: "This should remind us all once again that when dissent turns to violence, it invites tragedy."[53] Nixon's lack of sympathy for the Kent State victims or their families offended many Americans. Within days students at 450 colleges and universities were on strike. Governors of sixteen states called out the National Guard to quell campus disturbances.

Other tragedies soon followed. On May 7, police at the University of Buffalo in New York wounded four students. Six blacks were killed at a civil rights rally in Augusta, Georgia. And at Jackson State College in Jackson, Mississippi, highway patrolmen shot at demonstrators, killing two black students and wounding twelve. Across the nation, many Americans watched these unfolding events with horror. They could not believe U.S. troops and law enforcement officers were now shooting the nation's youth.

Others were not so sympathetic. Many conservative Americans blamed antiwar protesters for creating conditions that led to the shootings. Millions still supported the president and considered any criticism of American involvement in Vietnam as unpatriotic, if not treasonous. On May 20, one hundred thousand pro-war activists, many of them construction workers whose wrath against the demonstrators had been aroused during the Johnson years, now demonstrated in New York to show their support for Nixon and to counteract peace rallies.

By now few doubted that Nixon's handling of the war had ignited old passions and pitted Americans against each other. For months, more riots, rallies, and demonstrations shook the country. Trouble also brewed in Congress. During the spring several lawmakers in Congress introduced bills that required troop withdrawals from Southeast Asia and restrictions on the president's power to wage war. Though most of these attempts failed, one did become law: it barred U.S. ground troops from entering Cambodia or Laos.

Disaster in Laos

This restriction meant U.S. troops could not invade Laos when a high concentration of Communist troops amassed in that country in early 1971. In the wake of the Cambodia invasion, North Vietnam had moved many of its supply operations to Laos. And now American and South Vietnamese officials feared that the Communists were preparing for a major attack.

In February, the ARVN plunged alone into Laos to crush these preparations by

A Communist Woman at the Front

Karen Gottschang Turner's *Even the Women Must Fight* focuses on interviews with Vietnamese women who fought for North Vietnam. This excerpt from the book contains the recollections of Le Thi Linh in 1996.

1968 was a terrible year. My mother didn't want me to go to the front. But my sister had been killed and my two brothers wounded by an American bomb. I wanted to fight to avenge my family. When my workplace, the Ministry of Communications, called for volunteers, I was ready to go. I was eighteen years old. We walked in a group of 500 young people south, to an area at the battlefield near Hue. There, we worked in groups of five, in our case, three men and two women.

Because we handled top-secret information by radio, we could have no contact with anyone outside. We had to build tunnels to live in and to grow our own food, and because our equipment could give us away, we had to move at least three times a month to escape air raids. We couldn't cook because the smoke would betray us to the American planes and helicopters, and so sometimes we ate grass, we were so hungry. In order to keep the lines open, we would go for days without food when the fighting was fierce. We shared the work equally, according to our best abilities. We had to. Very little news from home ever reached us. I had one letter from my boyfriend, and we read it over and over again. We lived this way for six years.

A North Vietnamese girl stands guard over a downed U.S. airman. Women often fought to avenge the death or wounding of family members.

destroying the Ho Chi Minh supply trail. This was the first big test of Vietnamization. Backed only by U.S. air support, South Vietnamese troops strove to prove they could fight their own battles. They failed. Worse yet, they retreated with Communists in hot pursuit. South Vietnam's losses may have been as high as 50 percent. Vietnamization had not worked.

Disgust with the war grew in the United States. In March, a nationwide poll showed that support for Nixon's handling of the war had slipped to 34 percent. More bills appeared in Congress that demanded an end to U.S participation. The Nixon administration suffered another blow on June 13 when the *New York Times* released transcripts of a comprehensive secret study of the war commissioned by the Johnson administration. Even though these so-called "Pentagon Papers" revealed nothing personally embarrassing to Nixon, the president was nonetheless infuriated. For one thing, the study revealed that the government and the military had deliberately misled the American people about the true nature of the war. Nixon feared skepticism towards a previous administration could be transferred to him and his administration. He and Kissinger also worried that

publication of secret information might jeopardize ongoing negotiations if the Communists became convinced Americans could not keep secrets.

More bad news for Nixon arrived that summer when a special commission that he had appointed to study turmoil on the nation's colleges and universities concluded with a recommendation to the president that said:

> Nothing is more important than an end to the war in Indochina. Disaffected students see the war as a symbol of moral crisis in the nation which, in their eyes, deprives even law of its legitimacy. Their dramatic reaction to the Cambodian invasion was a measure of the intensity of their moral recoil.[54]

Failure to end the war and solve other social problems, warned the commission, meant "the very survival of the nation will be threatened. A nation driven to use the weapons of war upon its youth, is a nation on the edge of chaos."[55] But how to pull the nation out of Vietnam without assuring the destruction of South Vietnam was left to Nixon to figure out.

Chapter 7

Collapse and Withdrawal

The departure of all U.S. troops from Cambodia by June 30, 1970, demonstrated that Nixon had not permanently widened American involvement in the war. However, many problems had only grown worse because of the American incursion. The bombing in Cambodia caused vast destruction and killed thousands of Cambodians. The raids also generated intense hatred among the Khmer Rouge, who sought revenge by slaughtering anyone who supported the Cambodian government or the Americans.

Similar horrors were underway in Laos, where the CIA had secretly supported a right-wing dictatorship set up to combat another Communist movement, the Pathet Lao, that sought to gain control of the country. U.S. warplanes had bombed suspected enemy targets in Laos for years, obliterating homes, pagodas, and other buildings, and killing thousands. Writes American Fred Branfman, author and former resident of Laos:

Over 25,000 attack sorties [missions] were flown against the Plain of Jars [an undeveloped area of Laos strewn with huge ancient stone jars of unknown origin] from May 1964, through September, 1969; over 75,000 tons of bombs were dropped on it; on the ground, thousands were killed and wounded, tens of thousands driven underground, and the entire aboveground society leveled.[56]

Now Laos was a disaster. The bombing also did nothing to dissuade North Vietnam. Its troops, along with the Viet Cong, showed no signs of departing South Vietnam. Nor had they given up their goal of seizing Saigon. Instead, they simply waited for the Americans to leave.

Vietnamization's Final Phase

Until that day came, American advisers busily trained South Vietnamese units to defend themselves. In addition, the United

U.S. warplanes release their bombs over Laos. Despite their severity, the air strikes did nothing to dissuade North Vietnam.

Among the most controversial of all Vietnamization efforts was the CIA's Phoenix Program. Primarily an intelligence-gathering effort, the program's paid agents in Vietnam's villages identified and arrested suspected Viet Cong fighters, sympathizers, or collaborators. Supporters of the program claimed the plan made villages more secure and greatly depleted enemy ranks. Opponents, however, argued that it promoted murder, graft, and corruption. Of the 19,534 Viet Cong arrested under Phoenix, 6,187 were killed. Critics also charged that overzealous agents falsely accused innocent people in order to meet monthly quotas or extort payments for their release.

Vietnamization provoked other complaints. Many South Vietnamese believed the program was unfair because they now had to do most of the fighting and dying. Others felt betrayed by the gradual American pullout and held the United States responsible for much of the great disruption to their nation.

Many Americans also thought Vietnamization was a mistake. Some argued the ARVN was no match for the Communists. They believed that without military help from the United States, South Vietnam was certain to collapse. Many U.S. military advisers also believed most South Vietnamese lacked the education and technological expertise to operate and main-

States continued to supply naval, air, and logistical support to the ARVN, including massive shipments of new rifles, grenade launchers, machine guns, and hundreds of new helicopters. The United States sent weapons to Vietnam's territorial forces, or home guards, made up of villagers trained to defend their communities from the Viet Cong.

tain the high-tech weaponry given to them by the Americans.

The ARVN itself was plagued with problems. Among them were growing religious disputes between Catholics and Buddhists. There were also social-class conflicts. Vietnamese officers, for instance, traditionally came from the upper economic levels of Vietnamese society and looked down upon enlisted men from the countryside.

The ARVN suffered chronic morale problems. As American troops and their allies left Vietnam, the South Vietnam government had to increase the size of its own armed forces. To do this, the government drafted young men into the army when they were eighteen and planned to keep them until their fortieth birthday if needed. Most ARVN soldiers were also underpaid and received the equivalent of forty dollars a month. Because of these conditions, growing numbers of South Vietnamese deserted during the Nixon years. In 1969, 125,000 men abandoned the ARVN, and in 1970 the number increased to 150,000.

Deteriorating Morale Among U.S. Troops

The ARVN was not alone in having troubles. By 1971, U.S. military commanders also faced

major problems among their own troops. Among the most serious were those of leadership. By this time, the antiwar movement had taken its toll on the number of qualified young men willing to serve as officers in Vietnam. In 1960, the ROTC produced 230,000 new officers. But that number had

An American military adviser teaches an ARVN soldier how to use a grenade launcher. Many thought that the South Vietnamese troops lacked the education and expertise to operate the weapons given them.

dropped to 123,000 in 1969. To make up for the shortage, the army lowered its standards. Consequently, many new officers lacked the professionalism, intelligence, dedication, and training needed to lead men into battle. Making matters worse, many combat-hardened troops resented the arrival of inexperienced officers and suspected them of ordering dangerous and unnecessary missions merely to boost their own military careers.

Other rifts developed among U.S. troops. Career-minded enlisted men were often at odds with draftees who despised military life. Bitter animosity that reflected the racial turmoil in the United States erupted between whites and blacks. Race relations between Americans and the Vietnamese also worsened during the Nixon era. Many war-scarred GIs were unable to separate their hatred of their enemy from those they protected. To many Americans all Vietnamese were "gooks"—a derogatory name. Suspicion grew among many U.S. troops that too many South Vietnamese were ready and willing to betray Americans to the enemy. Growing numbers of disgruntled GIs thought they should not continue to risk their lives for what they saw as an ungrateful people. Some were also angry that after so many Americans had died in battle, their nation was preparing to leave Vietnam without a clear victory.

Without a strong motivation to fight, many GIs revolted. Some showed their unhappiness in symbolic ways. They wore armbands, beads, and other paraphernalia popular with antiwar demonstrators. Others were more aggressive. An alarming number of GIs began disobeying orders—especially those involving combat. The Department of the Army reported 382 court-martial cases involving "acts of insubordination, mutiny, and willful disobedience"[57] in 1970.

The most serious form of insubordination was "fragging." A slang expression derived from U.S. fragmentation grenades, fragging described any attack U.S. troops made against their own officers. Fragging's main purpose was to frighten officers into canceling combat orders. Attackers used grenades, knives, and guns. In 1970, GIs attacked 209 of their officers and killed 45.

Voice of Disillusionment

This passage from a letter written by Sergeant Phillip L. Woodall and quoted in *Time* reveals his disillusionment for the Vietnam War and the people he was asked to protect:

[My platoon leader died] fighting for a people who have no concern for the war, people he did not understand [who] knew where the enemy were, where the booby traps were hidden, yet gave no support. People that he would give portions of his food to yet would try to sell him a Coke for $1. People who cared not who the winner was—yet they will say he died for his country, keeping it free. Negative. This country is no gain that I can see, Dad. We're fighting, dying, for a people who resent our being over here. The only firm reason I can find is paying with Commie lives for U.S. lives.

Drug abuse also eroded military effectiveness. Many demoralized U.S. servicemen sought escape from the horror and tedium of Vietnam by using illicit drugs that were cheap and readily available from South Vietnamese civilians. A Department of Defense study reveals that as many as 50 percent of American troops used marijuana between 1969 and 1971. Heroin, an even more dangerous drug, also penetrated American camps and bases. In 1965, the U.S. Army arrested forty-seven men for drug violations; in 1969 that figure rose to eleven thousand. In 1971, fewer than five thousand soldiers were hospitalized for treatment of combat injuries, but more than four times that number received treatment for drug problems.

The combined impact of all these problems alarmed America's military leaders. Many believed that nothing less than a complete departure from Vietnam could stop the damage being done to America's armed forces. Nixon, however, was not yet ready to do this. He still sought a way for the United States to leave Vietnam with dignity.

A New Communist Offensive

Nixon did continue to order many troops to go home. By March 1972, an estimated seventy thousand U.S. personnel remained in Vietnam. Of these only six thousand were combat troops.

This reduction in U.S. forces meant the responsibility of defending Vietnam on the ground now rested with the ARVN. Its 1-million-man army was severely tested that spring when Communists launched another major attack, nicknamed the Easter offensive, on South Vietnam. Attacking in three successive waves, 120,000 North Vietnamese troops, along with thousands of Viet Cong swept into the northern provinces of South Vietnam, the Central Highlands, and an area north of Saigon. Stunned by the scale and size of the attack, the ARVN once again proved incapable of defending itself. Only American bombing and ground advisers kept the Communists from overwhelming the South Vietnamese.

Nixon retaliated by ordering the first sustained, massive bombing of North Vietnam since 1969. He also directed the U.S. military to mine the Haiphong harbor and other harbors to cut off Hanoi's supply lines from the Soviet Union. During the next six months, U.S. warplanes carried out forty-one thousand missions over North Vietnam.

On May 8, Nixon followed up the raids with words of conciliation. He announced that if North Vietnam agreed to release all American prisoners of war and to abide by a cease-fire, he would withdraw all remaining U.S. troops from Vietnam within four months. Nixon also stated that the Vietnamese people should negotiate their own solutions to their problems. What perhaps motivated him to make these remarks was a desire to end the war before the presidential election in the fall.

Nixon's open willingness to withdraw alarmed officials in South Vietnam. But the

Aircraft such as these U.S. Navy attack planes were used to mine Haiphong harbor in 1972.

Communists were also worried. For one thing, North Vietnam's allies, China and the Soviet Union, were now interested in improving ties with the United States. Hanoi's leaders wondered if improved relations meant North Vietnam's benefactors would abandon them. North Vietnamese officials also realized Nixon faced a weak rival for the presidency in the upcoming election and was sure to remain their adversary for four more years. They also understood they had not, and could not, militarily defeat the United States and ARVN as they had the French.

So, they agreed to negotiate in earnest. In July, Kissinger and North Vietnam's ne-gotiator, Le Duc Tho, met in Paris. By fall, they had worked out a draft of a peace agreement that called for a cease-fire and withdrawal of U.S. troops from Vietnam. In the document, the United States acknowl-edged the presence of fourteen North Viet-namese divisions in South Vietnam. Both sides agreed to exchange prisoners of war. The agreement also called for the estab-lishment of a new temporary government made up of representatives from Hanoi,

Saigon, and a neutral group to govern Vietnam until all parties worked out a more permanent solution. And to enhance South Vietnam's position in the wake of the American withdrawal, Nixon also initiated Operation Enhance Plus—a massive shipment of $2 billion in war materiel that eventually made South Vietnam's air force the fourth largest in the world.

Cautious optimism appeared during the months following the announcement of the agreement. "Peace is at hand,"[58] a confident Kissinger predicted on October 26. But he spoke too soon. Not all leaders welcomed the peace agreement. Despite American assurances of continued protection, Thieu was enraged by the agreement and angrily accused his American ally of abandoning South Vietnam and helping the enemy to overthrow his regime.

Thieu's words infuriated Nixon, who had been reelected in November and now wanted to end the war before his inauguration January 20. Desperate to keep the agreement from unraveling, the president informed Thieu that if he failed to sign the agreement the United States intended to sign a separate accord with the Communists. Some advisers in the White House gravely talked of ousting the South Vietnamese

leader from office if he upset the peace deal.

But Thieu held fast. The treaty was flawed, he insisted. For one thing, the agreement allowed 145,000 North Vietnamese troops to remain in South Vietnam. And this, he said, created a great peril for South Vietnam. Thieu declared that the agreement was vague about the

Henry Kissinger and North Vietnamese negotiator Le Duc Tho (left) met in Paris to work out a cease-fire in Vietnam.

role of the temporary government and who the neutral party would be that shared in governing.

Eventually Nixon backed down and asked Kissinger to renegotiate with the Communists over sixty-nine amendments Thieu wanted made to the agreement. Among other things, Thieu wanted North Vietnam to withdraw all its troops from South Vietnam and to recognize South Vietnam as a legitimate government. North Vietnam rejected all his ideas. Instead of reaching an accord, all sides stiffened their demands and bickered over the agreement into December.

At last Nixon lost all patience and demanded that North Vietnam negotiate "seriously" within seventy-two hours or reap serious consequences. When no acceptable negotiation was reached, he ordered Operation Linebacker Two—another bombing campaign—to commence on December 18. For the next eleven days, B-52s and other American aircraft flew three thousand bombing attacks on the highly populated areas between Hanoi and Haiphong. Nicknamed the "Christmas bombing," the raids provoked cries of protests from the mass media and governments around the world. According to the North Vietnamese, the raids killed 1,318 people in Hanoi and 305 in Haiphong. They also proved costly to the Americans, who lost twenty-six aircraft, including fifteen B-52s. In addition, ninety-three U.S. airmen were killed, captured, or reported missing.

At last, Hanoi signaled its readiness to renegotiate. Peace talks resumed on January 8, 1973. Ten days later Nixon ceased all bombing in North Vietnam. By January 23, 1973, Kissinger and Le Duc Tho worked out an agreement. Again Nixon informed Thieu that he must also sign the document or see the Americans strike a settlement on their own. This time Thieu relented and agreed to sign.

Although some U.S. officials believed that the bombing forced the Communists to negotiate seriously with Kissinger, the final treaty differed little from the version reached in October. Some political observers think Nixon had other goals in mind when he ordered Operation Linebacker Two. For one thing, the bombing reassured Thieu that the United States remained committed to the protection of South Vietnam. Secondly, it demonstrated to the Communists Nixon's willingness to punish North Vietnam if it violated the final treaty.

Though the war was at last really winding down, Nixon now had serious troubles at home. Scandal threatened his presidency. Americans learned that the president's reelection campaign officials had arranged a burglary of the Democratic Party headquarters in the Watergate office complex in Washington, D.C. In addition, Nixon's opponents in Congress threatened to cut off all funding for military operations in Southeast Asia.

On January 27, representatives of the United States, the South Vietnamese gov-

A civilian stands in a primitive bomb shelter in Hanoi during the Christmas bombing of 1972.

ernment, the North Vietnamese government and the People's Revolutionary Party of Vietnam (the new name for the political wing of the Viet Cong) signed the peace treaty. A cease-fire began the next day.

The treaty required the United States to withdraw its forces from Vietnam and dismantle its military bases there. In return, the Communists promised to return all American prisoners of war and give an official accounting of U.S. service personnel missing in action (MIA). All sides agreed to pull out all troops from Laos and Cambodia and to send no new troops or war materiels into South Vietnam. The

treaty also stipulated that both sides would retain the territories they controlled at the time of the cease-fire. Finally, the agreement stated that reunification of Vietnam would only be achieved by honest elections and other peaceful means. In addition, the United States pledged to continue economic aid to South Vietnam. Though Nixon also promised $3.25 billion in economic assistance to rebuild war-torn North

Vietnam, the U.S. Congress refused to honor this commitment.

For the most part, Nixon was satisfied with the peace agreement. It brought, he said, "Peace with honor in Vietnam."[59] But for many people the president's words rang hollow. Vietnam was only temporarily at peace. Despite negotiations, massive killing would continue for two more years. For many Vietnamese, such an outcome offered little honor for anyone.

The Fall of the South

After the signing of the peace treaty, most Americans considered their responsibility to South Vietnam to be over. Military aid from the United States tapered off as Communists returned U.S. prisoners of war. Meanwhile, U.S. troops continued to leave the country.

The American exit caused extreme hardships in South Vietnam. Not only was the country losing a powerful protector, it was also losing money. For many years, billions of U.S. dollars flowed into the local economy. Now this flow of money was drying up as the Americans departed. The result was massive unemployment and poverty.

As the Americans closed down their military operations, the Communists strengthened their grip on territories they had already seized in South Vietnam. By now they controlled 33 percent of the land in South Vietnam, though only 5 percent of the country's population. In these occupied areas, Communist forces built supply roads, laid down fuel lines to feed their growing number of mechanized units, and installed new surface-to-air missiles. Many of their ground soldiers now carried the most sophisticated weaponry available in the Communist world.

Despite agreeing to a cease-fire, the North Vietnamese were still determined to seize Saigon. In autumn 1973, Communist troops attacked airfields and storage facilities in South Vietnam. In the spring of 1974, they captured vast areas of the Mekong Delta. At the end of the year, the North Vietnamese and the Viet Cong launched a larger attack in Phuoc Long Province in the Central Highlands. President Thieu responded to the encroachment of Communist forces by ordering a pullback of ARVN troops from the Central Highlands to defend the remaining, more populated provinces.

But the ARVN was not in good shape to fight. Riddled with corruption, deteriorating morale, and high rates of desertion, South Vietnamese troops were unable to stop the Communist advance. Their failure sent a shock wave throughout South Vietnam. Millions of South Vietnamese were also dismayed that the United States failed to protect them during this clear violation of the peace treaty. "You have my assurance that we will respond with full force should the settlement be violated by North Vietnam,"[60] Nixon had promised Thieu in January. With a majority of Americans opposed to further involvement, it was now clear Nixon could not keep this promise.

A U.S. soldier gives the peace sign as he leaves Vietnam for home.

In addition, the four-nation International Commission for Control and Supervision (ICCS) responsible for monitoring compliance with the peace agreement proved powerless to stop the Communist attacks.

The Communist advance continued. Pleiku fell in March 1975. Next the ancient imperial capital city of Hue was captured. Communist forces swept over Da Nang on March 31 and headed toward their final prize—Saigon.

The Fall of Saigon

By April the Communists controlled nearly one half of South Vietnam's forty-four provinces and more than 50 percent of the country's population. Fearing reprisals and slaughter, tens of thousands of South Vietnamese packed their belongings and fled south and to the coast, where many swam or made their way in boats to U.S. Navy ships

anchored not far away. American officials believed the fall of Saigon was inevitable.

Though all U.S. combat troops were now gone, several thousand Americans remained in Vietnam, including diplomats, embassy guards, intelligence officers, military advisers, and Americans employed by various U.S. corporations, charities, and news organizations.

In early April, the United States launched an evacuation of Americans and any South Vietnamese in danger of being killed by the Communists once they took control. One of the immediate goals was to evacuate children, including orphans and children of mixed American and Vietnamese parentage. On April 4, an Air Force C-5A transport plane lifted off carrying 226 Vietnamese orphans—the first wave of two thousand children who were being flown to new homes in North America and Europe. Within minutes, the plane developed mechanical problems and crashed. Seventy-five children died, along with fifty American civilians and chaperons. Like so many other well-intentioned efforts in Vietnam, even a mercy flight ended in disaster.

South Vietnamese forces fought hard to stave off the Communists at Xuan Loc, a small provincial capital thirty-five miles east of Saigon. But they could not hold up against the Communist juggernaut. In a televised speech on April 21, President Thieu condemned the Americans for deserting his country; then he resigned and, along with many high-ranking South Vietnamese officials, fled the country. Soon heavy artillery was ready to pound Saigon.

When North Vietnamese gunners blasted Tan Son Nhut Air Base near Saigon on April 29, U.S. planners sped up the evacuation process. Now it was too late to rely on jet transport planes. Instead, the skies of Saigon darkened with evacuation helicopters that came to remove stranded Americans and non-Americans who faced retaliation or execution. Hour after hour, helicopters landed at Tan Son Nhut Air Base and on the roof of the U.S. embassy in Saigon to take evacuees to a flotilla of forty aircraft carriers, amphibious ships, and other vessels in the South China Sea. Asso-

ciated Press correspondent George Esper, who was in Saigon during the final evacuation, provides this description of the chaos aboard the U.S. command ship, the *Blue Ridge:*

> The air space above . . . [the ship] was jammed with South Vietnamese helicopters waiting to land and drop off evacuees.
>
> Eventually a system was worked out. One helicopter would land on the ship's pad and everybody would jump out. Then the crew would push it overboard, making room for the next one to land. But this took too much time. So helicopters began landing with their engines still running. After all the passengers were out, the pilots took off, swung out to sea and ditched the aircraft, jumping into the water from as high as 100 feet. Navy boats fished the pilots from the water.[61]

Meanwhile, American ships were also picking out of the sea thousands of refugees who had fled the mainland in boats, rafts, and other vessels.

The approach of Communist forces coupled with the frenetic evacuation efforts triggered a panic in Saigon. Thousands of men, women, and children stormed the American embassy in a desperate attempt to board the helicopters along with the departing Americans. Because there was not enough time or room to take most of them,

A Desperate Evacuation

In his book *The Eyewitness History of the Vietnam War: 1961–1975,* Vietnam War correspondent George Esper provides Associated Press photographer Neal Ulevich's personal remembrance of his experience trying to be evacuated from the American embassy during the fall of Saigon.

> We knew the Marines would take us in. We had to get in close. Thousands of Vietnamese were at the wall, hoping to climb over and into a helicopter. The Marines were pushing them back to keep the embassy from being overrun, allowing only Westerners and a few Saigon officials inside.
>
> Vietnamese began to crawl over the barbed wire on top of the wall, like commandos. One man caught his leg and fell. He dangled upside down, hanging by a lacerated leg.
>
> The Marines spotted us. Our group pushed nearer the wall. The crowd pressed closer. A youngster, perhaps 18, and half-American, clung desperately to my neck. "I will die if I stay," she cried out.
>
> Mothers held their children above the mass of people for Marines to take them inside. One of my cameras disappeared. Then my watch was gone. The Marines, still kicking Vietnamese, started grabbing the Westerners by their collars and hauling them up.
>
> [Once inside] it was easy. The embassy compound was in chaos, but a quiet man with a .45-calibre pistol in his belt led us to the inner court where Marines in combat gear guarded the walls.
>
> He led us into the building to make our way to the roof. Waiting in the corridors, we saw men calmly destroying code machines with hammers. The place was littered. Offices now were deserted.
>
> Telephones were ringing and no one was answering them.
>
> We were nearing the end.
>
> We heard the roar of the helicopter settling down on the embassy roof and we climbed the staircase. The Marine CH-46 was waiting when we emerged, its twin rotors turning great arcs in the drizzly grayness. Suddenly we were airborne and the lights of Saigon seemed like gems growing dimmer and smaller.
>
> In a while, more lights, red gems this time: the deck lights of the USS *Okinawa.* We were down. We were safe.

The last American helicopter to leave Vietnam loads evacuees on the roof of the U.S. embassy in Saigon.

Starting a New Life

In her essay on the website, "Fall of Saigon," Tran Ngo, who came to the U.S. in 1990, tells of her traumatic move to the United States:

After the Communists took over South Vietnam in 1975 people lost their freedom and became very poor. Also, students whose fathers had been officers were not allowed to go to the university even if they had high grades. The parents who had kids in high school were very worried and at that time I was seventeen years old. Many times I saw my mom look at me and sigh.

One day when I got home from school, I saw my mom talking anxiously to my uncle and a stranger. After they left my mom looked at me and said, "How would you feel if you lived alone?" In a second my ears felt like there were some ants crawling in there and my heart beat faster and faster. I asked, "What happened, Mom?" At first she didn't answer me, she just gave me a big hug. Then she said, "You are growing up. You have to know how to take care of yourself. I'll send you overseas." My body could not stand up I was so sad. I felt that heaven was falling. I cried a lot and couldn't sleep that night.

I knew my mom also felt sad like me. But after much thought, I realized that my mom was going to send me overseas because she loved me. She didn't want me to have a poor life. She wanted me to have a good education and a free life.

I'll always respect her for thinking of what was best for me even though she was miserable herself because my dad was in a concentration camp. I try to be a good kid and make her proud of me.

U.S. Marine guards had the grim duty of keeping throngs of sobbing, screaming Vietnamese away from the helicopters. Often, they had to beat their former allies back with their rifle butts.

As the end neared, many South Vietnamese police, youth, and soldiers looted the American compound. They stole cars, stereos, office equipment, furniture, and anything else that had value on the black market. Finally, at 7:52 A.M. on April 30, the last helicopter lifted off, leaving behind tens of thousands of people in Saigon to face the advancing enemy. Communist rockets soon struck the city, as petrified inhabitants of Saigon awaited the enemy's imminent arrival.

Surrender was left to the man who replaced Thieu—Duong Van Minh, now the acting president and one of the conspirators who overthrew Diem in 1963. About 10 A.M., Minh announced South Vietnam's unconditional surrender. Two hours later, Viet Cong and North Vietnamese troops marched proudly into Saigon. Alongside them came a fleet of tanks, trucks, and armored vehicles. Communist soldiers hoisted the red, blue, and yellow flag of the National Liberation Front over the presidential palace.

At last, the thirty-year-long Vietnam War was over. As Ho Chi Minh had once expected, the day of triumph had arrived when the Americans grew weary of war.

★ Epilogue ★

Legacies of War

Though the war was over, it haunted Americans for decades. Millions of Americans grieved for loved ones killed or hurt in Vietnam. Nearly fifty-eight thousand Americans died in the conflict; three hundred thousand were wounded. Several thousand GIs were reported missing in action (MIA). Others were believed to be held in Vietnamese prisons.

Millions of Americans remained angry and distrustful toward their government for its role in the war that killed 2.5 million Vietnamese, Cambodians, Laotians, Frenchmen, and Americans and their allies. Of these deaths, six hundred thousand were civilians. These misgivings contributed to a widespread antigovernment bias that grew stronger in the coming decades. Others experienced a different kind of remorse. Memories of American sailors pushing helicopters into the sea as Communist troops closed in on Saigon lingered for many as a shameful reminder of American betrayal of the South Vietnamese.

The treatment of Vietnam veterans also caused division in the postwar era. Though many Americans praised U.S. fighting men, others, including older veterans from previous wars, scorned them for failing to win. Recalls Dale Todd, a navy combat photographer in Vietnam in 1966 and 1968:

> Vets from World War II and Korea called Vietnam vets crybabies. But they weren't in a position to understand what we went through. To them the enemy was a guy in uniform on the other side of the line; they didn't have as enemy a farmer in the field, or a woman walking down the road with a bicycle. They didn't have to shoot children walking up with a hand grenade.[62]

Unlike in previous wars, most Vietnam War veterans did not receive huge welcome parades when they came home. Nor did they return with large groups of GIs and

105

have a chance to discuss their ordeals. Instead, most flew back alone to the United States within a few days of completing their tour of duty in Vietnam. Here they often met hostility or indifference from their fellow citizens. As a result of their traumas, many veterans readjusted badly to civilian life. Some never fit in. As many as twenty thousand veterans committed suicide in the postwar years. They also experienced high unemployment and prison rates for decades. Many also suffered from posttraumatic stress disorder, an ailment whose symptoms included involuntary memories, recurring nightmares, depression, and anxiety.

Thousands of American veterans received compensation from their government for illnesses—including various cancers and Hodgkin's disease—they claim are linked to their exposure to Agent Orange, the defoliant used in Vietnam. In February 2000, Vietnamese officials claimed that the millions of gallons of Agent Orange sprayed on their country did vast environmental damage, killed or injured four hundred thousand people, and contributed to at least half a million cases of birth defects. Many scientists, however, refute all these claims.

Perhaps the most controversial issue in the postwar years centered on the question of amnesty for draft evaders and deserters. An estimated 495,689 GIs fled from American bases in the United States, Europe, and Southeast Asia during the war. Although 90 percent returned to duty, between 32,000 and 50,000 did not. Many of these deserters joined the tens of thousands of exiles who evaded the draft and sought asylum abroad. At the end of the war, the nation debated what should be done about them. Should they receive conditional or full amnesty—a dropping of criminal charges—as Americans had at the end of the Civil War? Should they be given a full pardon—an official forgiveness for an offense? Or were they traitors and cowards who deserved prison sentences?

Many disillusioned Vietnam veterans ended up in prison after returning home. This one was arrested for bank robbery.

U.S. president Gerald Ford addressed these disturbing questions in 1974 when he granted conditional amnesty for evaders and deserters who agreed to do two years of public service work. The plan proved controversial: Many Americans thought it was too lenient, while others wanted unconditional amnesty. In any case, few accepted the offer.

Ford's successor, Jimmy Carter, provoked even more controversy in January 1977 when he ordered a full and unconditional pardon for most men who evaded the draft. Carter's plan, however, did not extend to deserters or those who received dishonorable discharges.

Continued Trouble in Vietnam

American anguish over the war intensified as terrible events unfolded in Southeast Asia. In Vietnam, Communist victors imprisoned hundreds of thousands of captives in forced labor camps, where they received harsh, rigorous teaching from the Communists who sought to brainwash them with the ideals of Communism. Many heartbroken South Vietnamese died from the brutal conditions.

Conditions were even worse in Cambodia. In 1975, the fanatical Communist faction—the Khmer Rouge—seized power and went on a massive killing spree. Under the leadership of Pol Pot, the Communists may have exterminated 1.2 million Cambodians, making the slaughter the worst case of genocide at the time since World War II. In 1978, Vietnam invaded Cambodia,

General Westmoreland Places Blame

In this passage, excerpted from *The National Experience: A History of the United States* by John M. Blum and others, General William C. Westmoreland, in 1976, blamed President Johnson and others for the American failure in Vietnam.

Despite the long years of support and vast expenditure of lives and funds, the United States in the end abandoned South Vietnam. There is no other way to put it. . . . After introduction of American combat troops into South Vietnam in 1965, the war still might have been ended within a few years, except for the ill-considered policy of graduated response against North Vietnam. Bomb a little, stop it awhile to give the enemy a chance to cry uncle, then bomb a little more but never enough to really hurt. That was no way to win. Yet even with the handicap of graduated response, the war still could have been brought to a favorable end following defeat of the enemy's Tet offensive in 1968. The United States had in South Vietnam at that time the finest military force—though not the largest—ever assembled. Had President Johnson provided reinforcements, and had he authorized the operations I had planned in Laos and Cambodia and north of the DMZ, along with intensified bombing and the mining of Haiphong Harbor, the North Vietnamese would have broken. But that was not to be. Press and television had created an aura not of victory but of defeat, and timid officials in Washington listened more to the media than to their own representatives on the scene.

ousted the Khmer Rouge, and set up a puppet government. China, angered by Vietnam's actions against an ally, attacked Vietnam, only to exit weeks later after meeting strong resistance.

Neighboring Laos was also in shambles. Here the Pathet Lao, another Communist-led guerrilla movement, waged war against a pro-American government put into power by the CIA in 1959. Between 1954 and 1960, the United States poured $300 million into Laos to thwart the spread of Communism. But that effort failed. Now the Pathet Lao controlled the country. Soon this rural Southeast Asian country too became a land of brutal concentration camps.

Millions of refugees fled these oppressive regimes. Fearing for their lives, Vietnamese, Laotians, Cambodians, and members of various ethnic groups such as Chinese and the Hmong—a mountain tribe whose men fought alongside the Americans—flooded into Thailand and China. Others took to the sea. In overcrowded, unsafe vessels, refugees known as "boat people" sought asylum in other Asian nations such as the Philippines, Malaysia, and Indonesia. Most refugees, however, were turned away to languish on the open sea. With nowhere to go, thousands perished from disease, drowning, starvation, and murder at the hands of pirates. At last, the United Nations stepped in and relocated tens of thousands of boat people to several Western nations, including the United States.

A Chastened Nation

The plight of the refugees, along with many other daily reminders of the war, traumatized Americans. Many wondered if their nation had lost its nerve to wage war, even in its own vital interest. As late as 1991, President George Bush tread cautiously when he sought public approval of his decision to send U.S. armed forces into the Persian Gulf to protect American oil interest. He promised the action would not result in another war like the one in Vietnam.

Although the United States took military action in foreign lands in the years following the Vietnam War, the missions were usually short-lived and limited. One reason for these reduced military roles is that modern presidents have had to contend with the War Powers Resolution, passed in 1973 by the U.S. Congress. This legislation allows a president to send troops abroad, but Congress must be notified within forty-eight hours of this action. In addition, the president may not keep the troops overseas for more than sixty days without congressional approval. Finally, Congress may order the troops home at any time.

Since 1973, American political and military leaders have tried to use various lessons of the Vietnam War to guide the nation on how and when to use military force. On one idea there is consensus: as Caspar Weinberger, secretary of defense in the Reagan administration in the early 1980s, put it, "Before the U.S. commits combat forces abroad, there must be some

Voyage of Death

In her memoir *Sensing the Enemy,* Lady Borton, a Quaker volunteer from the United States, chronicles her experiences as health administrator for the Malaysian island of Pulau Bidong that served as a temporary way station for Vietnamese boat people in 1980. This excerpt reveals the daily horror faced by thousands of refugees:

One morning an oil supply ship arrived with 352 new refugees and 2 corpses. A total of 28 passengers had died in route. The landing barge was a chaos of humanity: people picking up small children, people fainting, empty stretchers arriving, filled ones leaving. Patients occupied every hospital cot, sometimes two or three to each. All morning and afternoon I bathed toddlers and sponged the faces of children, young women and old men. I spooned water into mouths. The lips were bloated and chapped, the cheeks were dark and cracking. The eyes stared.

On the floor of the children's ward, toddlers curled inside their mothers' arms. One woman, whose husband had been among the twenty-eight, held a naked baby to her breast. Over each of her thighs climbed a naked toddler. Purple bubbles crusted the children's bodies. The mother shifted her baby from one breast to the other. During the trip she'd collected her toddler's urine and drunk it in order to nurse the infant.

By evening the dead were buried and the living settled. Nine men, who'd been accused of killing the twenty-eight, were safely confined inside the barbed-wire-encircled guards' compound. Several passengers had pointed at the nine men: "Viet-cong—Vietnamese Communist," they said. Others called the men gangsters. Some—and they were the ones I tended to believe—

said that during the trips there'd been frightening brawls over sips of water.

Whatever happened, it was clear from the crowd rumbling all day outside the compound that the lives of the nine men inside were endangered.

Several Vietnamese refugees are rescued and brought aboard a cargo ship.

reasonable assurance that we will have the support of the American people . . . and Congress."[63]

Healing the Wounds

Though the Vietnam War remained a divisive issue for decades, many of the wounds in American society ultimately began to heal. Today, millions of visitors to Washington, D.C., pay homage at a haunting black-granite memorial wall, inscribed with the names of Americans who died in Vietnam. Nearby are imposing, sculpted bronze figures representing the American men and women who served in Vietnam. Many who visit these memorials experience a powerful purging of emotions that helps them cope with the memories of a troubled time.

Some Americans wanted to do more for the Vietnam veterans. In the late 1980s, many communities staged belated but well-intentioned "welcome back" parades. The biggest took place in Chicago in 1986. Says Jim Williams, who served in Vietnam with the Army Assistant Helicopter Company from 1965 to 1967: "I appreciated it. I don't

Family members mourn a relative at the Vietnam memorial wall in Washington, D.C. Nearby stands a statue representing the American men who served in Vietnam.

know if it's a fix-all, but it was a very welcome gesture not only for me but for the 200,000 guys with me . . . and the 350,000 in the crowd. There were probably just as many people in the crowd who needed that parade as much as those marching in it. You could see it in people's eyes."[64]

International wounds were slower to heal. For decades, relations between the United States and Vietnam were bad. But by 1997, normal ties were restored, as trade and cultural exchanges increased.

Despite this improvement, Vietnam at the end of the twentieth century remained a poor country ruled by a Communist dictatorship. Neighboring Cambodia, now rid of the terrors of Pol Pot and the Khmer Rouge, struggled warily toward democracy. According to the U.S.-based watchdog organization the Laos Human Rights Council, the Communist party in Laos killed three hundred thousand Laotians in the past two decades and still rules with a deadly hand.

Such is the legacy of France's takeover of much of Indochina more than a century ago. Though the French are gone, something of the French era remains unchanged—the cruel repression of millions of people in Southeast Asia.

⋆ Notes ⋆

Introduction: America's Longest War

1. Quoted in William A. Henry III, "Richard Nixon's Tough Assessment," *Time*, April 15, 1985, p. 48.

Chapter 1: The Roots of American Involvement

2. Quoted in Robert Goldston, *The Vietnamese Revolution.* Indianapolis: Bobbs-Merrill, 1972, p. 51.
3. Quoted in Goldston, *The Vietnamese Revolution*, p. 54.
4. Quoted in George Esper and the Associated Press, *The Eyewitness History of the Vietnam War: 1961–1975.* New York: Ballantine Books, 1983, p. 6.
5. Quoted in the Editors of Time-Life Books, *Turbulent Years: The 60s.* Alexandria, VA: Time-Life Books, 1998, p. 110.
6. George Seldes, ed., *The Great Thoughts.* New York: Ballantine Books, 1985, p. 187.
7. Quoted in Goldston, *The Vietnamese Revolution*, p. 100.

Chapter 2: The United States Takes Charge

8. Quoted in Esper and the Associated Press, *The Eyewitness History of the Vietnam War*, p. 16.

9. Quoted in Stanley Karnow, *Vietnam: A History.* New York: Viking, 1983, p. 280.
10. Quoted in Esper and the Associated Press, *The Eyewitness History of the Vietnam War*, p. 33.
11. Quoted in Karnow, *Vietnam: A History*, p. 292.
12. Quoted in Spence C. Tucker, *Vietnam.* Lexington: University Press of Kentucky, 1999, p. 101.

Chapter 3: Johnson's War

13. Karnow, *Vietnam: A History*, p. 370.
14. Quoted in Esper and the Associated Press, *The Eyewitness History of the Vietnam War*, p. 43.
15. Quoted in Esper and the Associated Press, *The Eyewitness History of the Vietnam War*, p. 45.
16. Quoted in Karnow, *Vietnam: A History*, p. 372.
17. Quoted in Karnow, *Vietnam: A History*, p. 374.
18. Quoted in the Editors of Time-Life Books, *Turbulent Years*, p. 112.
19. Quoted in Karnow, *Vietnam: A History*, p. 395.
20. Quoted in Doris Kearns, *Lyndon Johnson and the American Dream.* New York: Harper and Row, 1976, pp. 251–52.

21. Quoted in Kearns, *Lyndon Johnson and the American Dream*, p. 260.

22. Quoted in Clark Dougan et al., *A Nation Divided*. Boston: Boston Publishing Company, 1984, p. 58.

23. Quoted in Kearns, *Lyndon Johnson and the American Dream*, p. 261.

24. Kearns, *Lyndon Johnson and the American Dream*, p. 275.

25. Quoted in Karnow, *Vietnam: A History*, p. 415.

Chapter 4: A Different Kind of War

26. Quoted in Joseph L. Galloway, "Fatal Victory," *U.S. News & World Report*, October 29, 1990, p. 32.

27. Galloway, "Fatal Victory," pp. 33–34.

28. Larry Phelps, interview with John M. Dunn, July, 1986.

29. Quoted in Tucker, *Vietnam*, p. 128.

30. Quoted in Esper and the Associated Press, *The Eyewitness History of the Vietnam War*, p. 93.

31. Quoted in Esper and the Associated Press, *The Eyewitness History of the Vietnam War*, p. 107.

32. Quoted in Esper and the Associated Press, *The Eyewitness History of the Vietnam War*, p. 104.

Chapter 5: The War at Home

33. Quoted in The Martin Luther King Jr. Papers Project at Stanford University, "Beyond Vietnam." www.stanford.edu.

34. Charles DeBenedetti and Charles Chatfield, *An American Ordeal: The Antiwar Movement of the Vietnamese War*. Syracuse, NY: Syracuse University Press, 1990, p. 109.

35. Quoted in DeBenedetti and Chatfield, *An American Ordeal*, p. 130.

36. Quoted in David Wallechinsky and Irving Wallace, *The People's Almanac*. Garden City, NY: Doubleday, 1975, p. 250.

37. Quoted in "Words of Hope and Horror," *Time*, April 15, 1985, p. 59.

38. Quoted in Joseph Boskin and Robert A. Rosenstone, eds., *Seasons of Rebellion, Protest and Radicalism in Recent America*. Lanhan, MD: University Press of America, 1980, p. 139.

39. Quoted in Kearns, *Lyndon Johnson and the American Dream*, pp. 348–49.

40. Quoted in Dougan et al., *A Nation Divided*, p. 130.

41. Quoted in Dougan et al., *A Nation Divided*, p. 132.

42. Quoted in Lance Morrow, "A Bloody Rite of Passage," *Time*, April 15, 1985, p. 23.

Chapter 6: Nixon Takes Charge

43. Quoted in Dougan et al., *A Nation Divided*, p. 10.

44. Quoted in Karnow, *Vietnam: A History*, p. 590.

45. Quoted in Stephen E. Ambrose, *Nixon: The Triumph of a Politician, 1962–1972*, vol. 2. New York: Simon & Schuster, 1989, pp. 275–76.

46. Quoted in Samuel Lipsman, Edward Doyle, and the Editors of Boston Publishing Company, *Fighting for Time*. Boston: Boston Publishing Company, 1983, p. 35.

47. Quoted in Ambrose, *Nixon*, p. 281.

48. Quoted in Ambrose, *Nixon*, p. 282.

49. Quoted in Vietnam News, "Hoà Chi Minh's Testament." Vnagency.com.vn/ 1999-08/29/stories/03.htm.

50. Quoted in Gorton Carruth, *What Happened When: A Chronology of Life and Events in America.* New York: Penguin Books, 1991, p. 997.

51. Karnow, *Vietnam: A History*, p. 597.

52. Quoted in Ambrose, *Nixon*, p. 345.

53. Quoted in Ambrose, *Nixon*, p. 350.

54. Quoted in 2000 May Fourth Task Force, "The Report of the President's Commission on Campus Unrest," September, 1970. www.Kent.edu/May4/Campus _Unrest _American_People.htm.

55. Quoted in 2000 May Fourth Task Force, "The Report of the President's Commission on Campus Unrest."

Chapter 7: Collapse and Withdrawal

56. Quoted in Howard Zinn, *A People's History of the United States.* New York: Harper & Row, 1980, p. 472.

57. Quoted in Lipsman et al., *Fighting for Time*, p. 100.

58. Quoted in Esper and the Associated Press, *The Eyewitness History of the Vietnam War*, p. 158.

59. Quoted in Esper and the Associated Press, *The Eyewitness History of the Vietnam War*, p. 158.

60. Quoted in Karnow, *Vietnam: A History*, p. 658.

61. Esper and the Associated Press, *The Eyewitness History of the Vietnam War*, pp. 198–99.

Epilogue: Legacies of War

62. Dale Todd, interview with the author, July 1986.

63. Quoted in "Lessons from a Lost War," *Time*, April 15, 1985, p. 40.

64. Jim Williams, interview with the author, July 1986.

★ Chronology of Events ★

1890

Ho Chi Minh is born.

1930

Ho helps form the Indochinese Communist Party.

1939

World War II begins; Ho returns to Vietnam.

1941

Ho forms the Viet Minh.

1941–1945

Viet Minh battle the French and Japanese.

1945

Japan surrenders to the United States; Ho's forces occupy Hanoi and proclaim a new republic; France seizes control of Saigon.

1946

French-Vietnamese war begins.

1946–1949

U.S. policy backs France.

1950

Truman administration recognizes French-controlled South Vietnam.

1954

Eisenhower administration increases financial aid to French combat efforts in Vietnam; Viet Minh defeat France at Dien Bien Phu; Geneva Peace Conference sets up Cambodia and Laos as independent nations; Vietnam split along the seventeenth parallel.

1955

U.S. military aid goes directly to South Vietnam, not France; Ho begins brutal land reform.

1956

French troops leave Vietnam; Diem elected chief of state and cancels reunification election; Hanoi backs rebels in South Vietnam.

1959

Diem cracks down on dissidents.

1960

North Vietnam announces support for overthrow of Diem's government.

1961

Kennedy becomes president; gives more aid to Diem.

1962

Kennedy increases U.S. military advisers in South Vietnam to twelve hundred.

1963

Viet Cong defeat ARVN at Ap Bac hamlet;

Diem cracks down on Buddhists; military coup kills Diem and his brother; assassin kills Kennedy; first major antiwar rally in New York.

1964

North Vietnamese patrol boats attack the USS *Maddox;* Gulf of Tonkin Resolution gives Johnson authority to attack North Vietnam; United States bombs Laos; Communists attack Bien Hoa Air Base; Viet Cong bomb American-occupied hotel in Saigon.

1965

Communists attack U.S. base at Pleiku; Johnson orders Operation Rolling Thunder and sends first combat troops into Vietnam; U.S. officials report victory at Ia Drang Valley; teach-ins occur at one hundred campuses; SDS sponsors first national protest in Washington, D.C.; thousands protest draft deferment changes; one hundred thousand in eighty cities attend International Day of Protest.

1966

Second International Day of Protest held in major cities.

1967

Westmoreland launches first large-scale search-and-destroy mission at Ben Suc; Spring MOBE protest attracts four hundred thousand.

1968

Giap orders the Tet offensive; American forces rout Communist troops; Johnson orders bombing halt and calls for negotiations; My Lai massacre occurs; student riots at Columbia University; Johnson refuses to run for reelection; antiwar riots at Democratic convention in Chicago; Nixon elected president.

1969

Communists launch a second Tet offensive; Nixon orders secret bombing of Cambodia; Vietnamization begins; Hanoi rejects Nixon's call for a bilateral withdrawal from Vietnam; Nixon announces troop withdrawals; Ho Chi Minh dies.

1970

Lon Nol ousts Sihanouk; Nixon orders invasion of Cambodia; more protests sweep the United States; National Guard soldiers kill four students at Kent State; new round of protests.

1971

Communists oust ARVN from Laos; the *New York Times* publishes *The Pentagon Papers;* U.S. troops leave Cambodia.

1972

Communist-based Easter offensive humiliates ARVN; Nixon orders new round of bombing; Kissinger and Le Duc Tho work out peace agreement; Thieu refuses to sign, negotiations break down; Nixon orders "Christmas bombings."

1973

Nixon stops bombing and negotiations resume; all parties sign peace treaty;

Communists violate treaty by attacking sites in northern areas of South Vietnam.

1974

Communist troops invade Mekong Delta and Central Highlands; Ford offers amnesty program.

1975

U.S. evacuates as Communist troops conquer all major cities in South Vietnam; Duong Van Minh surrenders South Vietnam to the Communists; the war ends; mass exodus of boat people refugees begins; U.S. Congress passes War Powers Resolution and cuts off funds to South Vietnam.

1977

Carter offers pardon to most American exiles.

1997

Vietnam and the United States restore diplomatic relations.

★ For Further Reading ★

David Bender and Bruno Leone, eds., *The Vietnam War: Opposing Viewpoints*. San Diego: Greenhaven Press, 1984. A collection of essays on controversial issues of the Vietnam War.

Edward F. Dolan Jr., *Amnesty: The American Puzzle*. New York: Franklin Watts, 1977. An interesting look at varying views concerning amnesty for draft evaders, deserters, and those who received dishonorable discharges during the Vietnam War.

E. B. Fincher, *The Vietnam War*. New York: Franklin Watts, 1980. A concise history of the war.

Susan Sheehan, *Ten Vietnamese*. New York: Alfred A. Knopf, 1967. A collection of well-written and interesting biographical sketches, based on personal interviews of Vietnamese civilians impacted by the fighting in Vietnam.

★ Works Consulted ★

Books

Bill Adler, ed., *Letters from Vietnam*. New York: E. P. Dutton, 1967. A compilation of correspondences from American servicemen and others of their experiences in Vietnam.

Stephen E. Ambrose, *Nixon: The Triumph of a Politician, 1962–1972*. Vol. 2 New York: Simon & Schuster, 1989. An informative and lively biography by a popular historian.

John M. Blum, William S. McFeely, Edmund S. Morgan, Arthur M. Schlesinger Jr., Kenneth M. Stampp, and C. Vann Woodward, *The National Experience: A History of the United States*, 6th ed. San Diego: Harcourt Brace Jovanovich, 1985. A college-level text book.

Lady Borton, *Sensing the Enemy: An American Woman among the Boat People of Vietnam*. Garden City, NY: Doubleday, 1984. A graphic and stunning account of a volunteer worker's personal experiences among the boat people in Malaysia.

Joseph Boskin and Robert A. Rosenstone, eds., *Seasons of Rebellion, Protest and Radicalism in Recent America*. Lanhan, MD: University Press of America, 1980. A collection of essays on various protest movements during the second half of the twentieth century.

Gorton Carruth, *What Happened When: A Chronology of Life and Events in America*. New York: Penguin Books, 1991. A chronological encyclopedia of historical facts about American history.

Charles DeBenedetti and Charles Chatfield, *An American Ordeal: The Antiwar Movement of the Vietnam War*. Syracuse, NY: Syracuse University Press, 1990. A captivating and comprehensive history of the antiwar movement.

Edward Doyle, Samuel Lipsman, Stephen Weiss, and the Editors of the Boston Publishing Company, *Passing the Torch: The Vietnam Experience*. Boston: Boston Publishing Company, 1981. A readable, detailed account of the final days of the French experience in Vietnam and how the United States became involved in the conflict.

Clark Dougan, Edward Doyle, Samuel Lipsman, and the Editors of Boston Publishing Company, *A Nation Divided*. Boston: Boston Publishing Company, 1984. A very readable account of the protest movement spawned by opposition to the Vietnam War.

George Esper and the Associated Press, *The Eyewitness History of the Vietnam War: 1961–1975*. New York: Ballantine Books,

1983. A lively firsthand account of the war, enriched with an abundance of photographs.

Editors of Time-Life Books, *Turbulent Years: The 60s.* Alexandria, VA: Time-Life Books, 1998. This vivid account of the turbulent 1960s contains a readable and richly illustrated overview of the Vietnam War.

Donald M. Goldstein, Katherine V. Dillon, and J. Michael Wenger, *The Vietnam War: The Story and Photographs.* Washington, D.C.: Brassey's. Enhanced by an abundance of photographs, this account is an informative, but at times opinionated, presentation of the major military events of the war. Written for the general reader.

Robert Goldston, *The Vietnamese Revolution.* Indianapolis: Bobbs-Merrill, 1972. A well-written, concise account of the war through the Johnson years.

Karen Gottschang Turner and Phan Thanh Hao, *Even the Women Fight: Memories of War from North Vietnam.* New York: John Wiley and Sons, 1998. This fascinating book by a Harvard scholar presents interviews and stories of the women who fought for North Vietnam.

Seymour M. Hersh, *My Lai 4: A Report on the Massacre and Its Aftermath.* New York: Random House, 1970. A gripping account of the massacre, by one of the nation's top investigative journalists.

Stanley Karnow, *Vietnam: A History.* New York: Viking, 1983. A highly acclaimed work by a top journalist who combined personal experience in Vietnam with solid scholarship to produce a readable, fascinating, and comprehensive history.

Doris Kearns, *Lyndon Johnson and the American Dream.* New York: Harper and Row, 1976. An extremely well written biography of Lyndon Johnson, with brilliant insights into the forces that shaped his policy on American involvement in Vietnam.

Samuel Lipsman, Edward Doyle, and the Editors of Boston Publishing Company, *Fighting for Time.* Boston: Boston Publishing Company, 1983. A well-written account of the war during Nixon's presidency.

Robert James Maddox, ed., *American History: Reconstruction Through the Present.* 10th ed. Guilford, CT: The Dushkin Publishing Group, 1989. A collection of articles on American history.

Jules Roy, *The Battle of Dienbienphu.* New York: Harper and Row, 1963. A well-documented, comprehensive history of the historic battle.

George Seldes, ed., *The Great Thoughts.* New York: Ballantine Books, 1985. A compilation of short passages of many of the greatest ideas in history.

Neil Sheehan, Hedrick Smith, D. W. Kenworthy, and Fox Butterfield, *The Pentagon Papers.* New York: Quadrangle Books, 1971. A fascinating summary of a top secret study undertaken by the Pentagon of the history of the U.S. role in the Vietnam War. Many of the revelations in these documents contradict beliefs about the war commonly held today.

Spence C. Tucker, *Vietnam*. Lexington: University Press of Kentucky, 1999. A concise, up-to-date history of the war, with an objective emphasis on the military aspects by a military historian.

David Wallechinsky and Irving Wallace, *The People's Almanac*. Garden City, NY: Doubleday, 1975. A popular reference book of unusual and interesting topics.

Howard Zinn, *A People's History of the United States*. New York: Harper & Row, 1980. An unorthodox history told from the perspectives that are often overlooked by mainstream writers.

Periodicals

Joseph L. Galloway, "Fatal Victory," *U.S. News & World Report*, October 29, 1990.

Robert Dreyfuss, "Apocalypse Still," *Mother Jones*, February 2000.

George J. Church, "Lessons from a Lost War," *Time*, April 15, 1985.

William A. Henry III, "Richard Nixon's Tough Assessment," *Time*, April 15, 1985.

"Words of Hope and Horror," *Time*, April 15, 1985.

Interviews

Connie Brawley. Interview by author. April 2000.

Dale Dodd. Interview by author. July, 1986.

Larry Phelps. Interview by author. July 1986.

Jim Williams. Interview by author. July 1986.

George Moore. Interview by author. July 1986.

Internet Sources

"Anti-War Movement," *The American Experience* (www.pbs.org). This episode of *The American Experience* series, found through the Public Broadcasting System website, offers a good summary of the antiwar movement.

"Beyond Vietnam," The Martin Luther King Jr. Papers Project at Stanford University. (www.stanford.edu). This site has a wealth of information about King, including his sermons and speeches on Vietnam.

"Fall of Saigon," (www.vmccd.cc.ca.us/mc/fall/default.html). This website, created by Marianne Brems, contains a collection of personal memoirs composed by Vietnamese exiles who experienced the Vietnam War.

"Hoà Chi Minh's Testament," Vietnam News (Vnagency.com.vn/1999-08/29/stories/03.htm). A Ho Chi Minh City website in English.

"Human Rights Violations and War in Laos," February 17, 1997, letter (http://home.earthlink.net/~Laohumrights/). An independent website that claims to track human rights abuses in Laos.

"The Report of The President's Commission on Campus Unrest, September 1970," posted by the 2000 May Fourth Task Force (www.Kent.edu/May4/Campus_Unrest_American_People.htm). The Task Force is a group set up to study the violence at Kent State in 1970.

✯ Index ✯

★ Picture Credits ★

Cover photo: © Bettmann/Corbis
Archive Photos, 9, 10, 14, 43, 51, 60, 63, 67
Archive France/Archive Photos, 20
Associated Press AP, 58
Terry Atlas/Archive Photos, 71
© Bettmann/Corbis, 7, 23, 31, 38, 52, 57, 65, 69, 76, 77, 79,
    81, 82, 91, 101, 103, 106
Express Newspapers/Archive Photos, 97
Express Newspapers/D082/Archive Photos, 109
© Hulton-Deutsch Collection/Corbis, 99
© Owen Franken/Corbis, 105, 110 (left)
Lyndon Baines Johnson Library, 35 (top), 37
Wolfgang Kaehler/Corbis, 110 (right)
National Archives, 11, 17, 22, 24, 28, 41, 45, 46 (both), 48, 54,
    92, 93, 96
Tim Page/Corbis, 85
Popperfoto/Archive Photos, 27
Russell Reif/Archive Photos, 68
© Reuters NewMedia Incorporated/Corbis, 35 (bottom), 87
Martha Schierholz/Joseph Paris Picture Archives, 12
U.S. Air Force, 61
© Nevada Weir/Corbis, 13

★ About the Author ★

John M. Dunn is a freelance writer and high school history teacher. He has taught in Georgia, Florida, North Carolina, and Germany. As a writer and journalist, he has published over 300 articles and stories in more than 20 periodicals, as well as scripts for audio-visual productions and a children's play. His books *The Russian Revolution, The Relocation of the North American Indian, The Spread of Islam, Advertising, The Civil Rights Movement, The Enlightenment,* and *Life During the Black Death* are published by Lucent Books. He and his wife live with their two daughters in Ocala, Florida.